MENTO

TO
DEVELOP
DISCIPLES
&
LEADERS

John Mallison

By the same author

How to Commence Christian Cells in the Local Church (1954)
Lay Witness Teams (1972)
Youth Outreach and Evangelism (1975)
How to Communicate Your Faith (1975)
The Small Group Series:
  1. *Guidelines for Small Groups* (1976)
  2. *Learning and Praying in Small Groups* (1976)
  3. *Keeping Group Life Vital* (1976)
  4. *Celling Youth and Adults* (1976)
Christian Lifestyle Discovery through Small Groups (1977)
Building Small Groups in the Christian Community (1978)
Creative Ideas for Small Groups (1978)
Survival Kit for Christian Disciples (1979)
Caring for People – Leaders and Participants Manuals (1979)
Nurturing New Disciples in Small Groups (1980)
Caring for New Christians (co-author with Dr Eddie Gibbs 1982)
Becoming a Follower of Jesus Christ (1983)
Growing Christians in Small Groups (1989)
Living as a Christian in Today's World (1990)
The Small-Group Leader (1996)

Contributor to:
Still Waters, Deep Waters (1987)
Preaching and Evangelism in Secular Australia (1989)
The NIV Serendipity Bible (1991)
The Best of GRID (1993)
Many Models One Aim (1994)

MENTORING

TO
DEVELOP
DISCIPLES
&
LEADERS

John Mallison

Scripture
Union

OPENBOOK
PUBLISHERS

Mentoring to Develop Disciples and Leaders is published by

Scripture Union	Openbook Publishers
Resources for Ministry Unit	205 Halifax Street
PO Box 77, Lidcombe	Adelaide, South Australia 5000
NSW 1825	

Distributed in the UK by Scripture Union
207-209 Queensway, Bletchley, Milton Keynes, Bucks MK2 2EB, England

First published October 1998
08 07 06 05 04 03 02 01 00 99   10 9 8 7 6 5 4 3 2

National Library of Australia
Cataloguing-in-Publication entry

Mallison, John.
Mentoring to develop disciples and leaders.

Bibliography.
Includes index.
ISBN 0 85910 895 3.

1. Mentoring in church work. 2. Discipling (Christianity).
3. Christian leadership. I. Scripture Union Australia.
II. Title.

253.7

Cover Design by Graeme Cogdell
Diagrams by Andrew Mallison
Printed by Openbook Publishers
205 Halifax Street, Adelaide, South Australia 5000   0284-99

To my first mentor,
my father

Edwin (Ted) S Mallison

engineer, Bible teacher, preacher, evangelist,
and equipper of emerging leaders

Introducing John Mallison

John Mallison has had extensive experience in mentoring Christian leaders, young and old, in all sections of the church throughout Australia and in numerous countries overseas. He now devotes himself almost entirely to modelling, teaching and promoting mentoring.

He is currently Director of Mentoring for the Australian Arrow Leadership Program, an initiative of Leighton Ford.

As an internationally known Christian educator, John Mallison is a specialist in enabling mainly the laity to develop personally and spiritually, and in equipping them for service. While serving as Director of Adult Education for the Uniting Church in NSW, he founded and directed the ELM Centre, their Lay Education Centre.

His broad parish ministry in Australia has spanned twenty-seven years, seventeen of which were spent full-time in rural, industrial and developing urban areas and ten years part-time in an experimental inner-city parish.

He now has his own training organisation called John Mallison Ministries.

He founded the Australian Small Group Network, a national movement involving all denominations aimed at maximising the impact of small groups upon the church and nation.

A prolific writer, his twenty-one books deal with the role of small groups in Christian community, evangelism, nurture of new disciples, Christian life-style development and pastoral care.

He has special skills and wide experience in cross-cultural ministry, having conducted training events in twenty-nine countries.

For more information about mentoring contact John Mallison at

John Mallison Ministries Inc
PO Box 5304, West Chatswood, NSW 2057, Australia
Website: www.mentoring.org.au

ACKNOWLEDGMENTS

Without the insights, assistance, encouragement and prayers of a large number of people, you would not be reading this book!

Gordon Dicker first encouraged me to reflect on my experiences and write this book. Many authors, Christian and secular, some of whom I have mentioned in the brief bibliography, have enhanced my thinking. The participants in the seminars on mentoring I have led over recent years, by their feedback, helped me develop some early drafts of sections of this book.

Those who have mentored me have provided good models on which to reflect and learn. My mentorees have helped me develop my mentoring skills, often at their expense!

Hope Cassidy, Edna Pontin and Lea Richards contributed greatly by their skilful editing. Many made helpful, critical comments on the final draft. My son, Paul, heads this list for his extensive work. Others include, John Allison, Bill Brown, Greg and Meryem Brown, Richard Condie, Gordon Dicker, Anne Gibbons, Brian Hill, John Lane, Brian Marks, Cliff Powell, Peter Ralphs, John R Reid, Ian Richardson, Les Scarborough and John U'Ren.

Those who have contributed material have been acknowledged in the text.

The graphics were prepared by my son, Andrew. My intercessors Ruth McDonald and Lester James and many other prayer partners faithfully undergirded this work in prayer over a long period. My secretary of many years, Mary Butler, has contributed very significantly to yet another of my books through her skills, wisdom and grace. My wife has patiently and prayerfully encouraged and supported me.

Last, but not least, my thanks to God for all his faithfulness and for calling me into this exciting ministry of mentoring.

We acknowledge with thanks the following permissions to quote: Accountability Questions prepared by Neil Cole and Robert E Logan, 1992–1995; Spiritual Issues Director's Guide, prepared by Greg and Meryem Brown.

FOREWORD

This book is the result of many years of effective ministry as a pastor, educator and denominational leader. John Mallison's ministry has been exercised in Australia and overseas and across many denominations. In recent years an increasing number of younger church leaders have come to him for advice and encouragement. In fact, he was discipling, or mentoring, long before he ever began to reflect on the processes involved. Some people may have been content to leave this ministry in an unstructured form; however the author is a leader in teaching how adults learn and how small groups function. It is this side of his multi-faceted ministry which has taken over and the book unveils a whole panorama of methods, skills and strategies. Each section has thought-provoking questions for individuals and groups.

There are two things which should be mentioned. The book is clear as crystal that Jesus Christ is the model and goal of personal growth and ministry. Everything in the book seeks to be related to this fundamental biblical emphasis.

In addition, the book draws on a wide range of recent literature on spirituality, how adults learn and counselling skills. In fact, I know that all the sections of the book were submitted to experienced people for advice. There is a lot of wisdom in these pages.

The book makes a unique contribution in our literature on pastoral care and especially of the care of leaders. I believe it to be a first-class resource book, and I am privileged to commend it.

Bishop John R Reid

CONTENTS

INTRODUCTION
A DOOR INTO THIS BOOK

L et me open the door, switch on the light and quickly walk you through this book and, as we go, make some explanations so you get an overview of what it contains.

THE FLOOR PLAN
A brief look at the Contents page helps get this book into perspective. This overview gives some idea of my core commitments in writing this book. I have sought to achieve the following:
- To show that mentoring is not an optional extra, if followers of Christ are to mature and fulfil God's purpose for them.
- To encourage every follower of Christ to take an interest in another's personal and spiritual growth (to 'watch over one another in love'). Mentoring others is not reserved for the giants of the faith!
- To emphasise that the foundation for effective Christian mentoring is a vital, growing relationship with Jesus Christ.
- To give a clear understanding of the various dimensions of mentoring and what is involved.
- To explain that mentoring can be done with varying degrees of intensity from a close friendship to a professional relationship, occasional wise words of encouragement and guidance to well-structured, regular meetings.
- To lay a sound biblical and theological basis for mentoring.
- To provide some practical guidelines for both mentors and mentorees.

- To emphasise that mentoring is essentially experience-based learning to which reflection is central.
- To help especially leaders see the broad possibilities for mentoring. To provide case studies of some options and enable them to develop mentoring networks in their churches or organisations.
- To present Jesus Christ as our prime mentoring model.

WHO THIS BOOK IS FOR

I have written this book for a broad cross-section of readers, including:

- **Potential mentors/mentorees**, who want to know how to go about it and how to begin.
- **Mentors** who want to improve their performance by honing their skills and discovering new ideas.
- **Team leaders** who want to build their teams through mentoring.
- **Supervisors** in bible and theological college supervised field education programs, who want to maximise their mentoring.
- **Church and para-church leaders** who want to implement their own mentoring networks.
- **Trainers** who want a sound educational resource to equip mentors.
- **Friends** who want their friendships to be more effective in helping each other grow personally and spiritually.

WHAT THIS BOOK CAN DO FOR YOU

It will:

- help you catch a vision of mentoring
- encourage you to begin
- provide practical know-how
- help you experience the potential of reflection for learning from the experiences through which God has taken you
- enable you to find a mentor or a mentoree
- equip you to build effective teams
- open your eyes to how churches and Christian organisations can be transformed through organised mentoring.

How the study/training dimension works

The Study Guides: Most sections of this book have study guides.

- **The personal reflection.** This segment is central to facilitating self-understanding and insight. The outcome for a mentored person is not only to become a Christ-centred disciple, but a reflective Christ-centred disciple. It can be used on your own to help make more of your reading of the text. If you are using it with others, you will need to make notes.
- **Group work** can be done with one other person or a small group of ideally six or eight people. Your reading of the text and personal reflection provides the basis of the group work. There will be little, if any, lecturing. If other groups are involved, there will be times for groups to share their findings with each other.

The Trainer's Guide: This provides a recommended program and clear guidelines for the trainer.

The Group Covenant: The commitment of each participant is sought to be maximised through agreement to this covenant.

Resources which have moulded my thinking

The **bibliography** towards the end of this book lists only some of the Christian and secular books which have influenced me.

My major resource, in addition to the Bible, has been my reflection on my own varied experiences, personal and spiritual, and in mentoring others. Indeed, I hope that you, the readers, will become aware of the powerful nature of reflection as you note how much of the practical know-how has grown out of my own extensive reflection. It has been of profound benefit to me personally, in writing this book, to be compelled to process my experiences and recognise how God has been at work in my life, prompting, equipping, inspiring, shaping, empowering in ways of which I was not aware, until I set aside time for intensive reflection.

CHAPTER 1

INTRODUCING MENTORING

MY JOURNEY IN MENTORING

Mentoring is a reasonably recent term, especially in Christian circles. But what it seeks to describe has been the focus of Christian community since its inception. Paul sums it up well in his letters to his mentorees Timothy and Titus. It involves developing disciples through encouragement and sound instruction based on God's word (Titus 2:6,15) and the formation of leaders (2 Tim 2:2).

Over many years I have had a most fulfilling and varied ministry. Mentoring has had an integral place in my work with others, but over the last fifteen years my passion for mentoring has become more and more intense, until now it is the most exhilarating aspect of my ministry – I love mentoring! I am passionate about mentoring not solely because it is so satisfying but because I never cease to be amazed at the great difference for good it can make in another's life.

For me, mentoring is not a recent discovery; it has been an indispensable part of my journey. I was greatly privileged to be born into a Christian home where Christ was central. My parents taught me to pray and nurtured me in the things of Christ. During the challenges I faced in my early theological studies, my father continually sought to keep me Christ-centred and Bible-based – occasionally there were some heavy discussions!

My wife, June, has always faithfully mentored our children. As they have matured, my own mentoring of them has become more significant (and theirs of me!). My ministry, as well as my personal life, has been so very greatly enhanced by June's perception and prayerful support.

In the early stages of my Christian life, the Scripture Union movement, through which I found Christ and then served as a voluntary worker, provided me with a few who discipled me.

Before entering the ministry, I did studies to prepare me as an industrial arts teacher and then, because of an attractive offer, switched to training as an electrical fitter. I experienced the effectiveness of coaching as an apprentice in a busy workshop, paired with skilled artisans.

My early years of ministry were greatly enriched by a number of ministers who took a personal interest in me. While serving part-time in a parish in the Blue Mountains, west of Sydney, Herbert Green met with me weekly to discuss my work. He showed great confidence in me, trusted me with big responsibilities, was full of encouragement and much of his wisdom laid a good foundation for later years. Each time I preached, there was a note of affirmation and encouragement from him left on the pulpit.

Gloster Udy was my long-term mentor. I first encountered him while I was preaching as a theological student. I was deeply impressed by his intense attention. His apparent interest drew the best out of me. At the conclusion, he was full of encouragement (although much later, I learnt it was my sincerity, not my homiletic skills, that won his heart!). That marked the beginning of a long-term mentoring relationship.

Not only did he encourage me to reflect on some innovative work I was doing in my parish with small groups, and to write about it, he even edited the manuscript and arranged for its publication. Then, through lecturing opportunities he organised, I quickly became known nationally.

Through his wise counsel, Bishop Jack Dain, a senior bishop of the Sydney Anglican diocese, was another great influence in my life and ministry. He opened up new areas of learning through sponsoring my attendance at a number of international gatherings which introduced me to world leaders. Over the years, our relationship grew into more one of mutual mentoring, as we shared openly and prayed together.

Not only the clergy but the whole Christian family of faith has influenced my life and ministry. Many lay people have inspired and challenged me by their wise guidance, strong faith and deep commitment to their Lord and to myself. They have been 'potters' moulding this clay vessel.

Although I have a couple of enriching peer mentoring relationships at present, my paramount experience in this aspect of mentoring was with a close friend, Bob Hillman, who contracted cancer in the prime of his dynamic ministry. We covenanted to pray together weekly, either face-to-face or by phone. This often necessitated calls from overseas during my frequent trips away. During our regular get-togethers, we shared with great openness and honesty. This deep bond lasted for the remaining eleven years of his life.

Mentoring others has always been an important aspect of my ministry. Very early in my ministry, I saw the importance of discipling those who made commitments to Christ, and sought to do that faithfully.

In most stages of my ministry, I have been responsible for heading teams of varying sizes. In these situations, I have sought to assess the levels of competency of each team member, varying the degree of my mentoring of each individual accordingly. It has always been a delight to observe in my teams the development in confidence and competence that takes place through appropriate encouragement, coaching, support and delegation of increased responsibility.

I now have a network of 140 leaders whom I mentor with varying degrees of intensity. They are scattered throughout Australia, across all denominations, and include some nationals living abroad. I meet regularly with a small number who live in Sydney. The others I keep in touch with by letter, phone and e-mail. When I visit their area during my frequent travels, I arrange to spend time with them. They all know I am available whenever they need a listening ear and they are frequently in my prayers.

I get sufficient positive feedback to know that, under God, these leaders are finding encouragement, direction and hope through having someone readily available to listen and support them.

One dynamic young leader, whom I mentor at a distance, experienced horrendous stress through persistent family difficulties and malicious criticism. He told me recently, 'The few hours you were able to spend to hear me out and pray with me marked a turning point for me (I now have hope and renewed confidence!)'.

—✳✳✳—

MENTORING (ITS ORIGIN AND MEANING)
THE ORIGIN OF THE WORD

The word 'mentoring' comes from Greek mythology. In Homer's *Odyssey*, Mentor was the wise and trusted companion and friend of Ulysses and the guardian of his house during his ten-year absence at the Trojan wars. He acted as teacher and adviser of Ulysses' son Telemachus, helping him to develop sound values, attitudes and behaviour so that he would mature to be an upright, wise and courageous adult.

DEFINITION
Christian mentoring is a dynamic, intentional relationship of trust in which one person enables another to maximise the grace of God in their life and service.

This definition applies to the three dimensions of mentoring dealt with in this book. It focuses on the heart of all Christian mentoring: a vital relationship with God.

SIGNIFICANT WORDS AND PHRASES IN THIS DEFINITION

- **Relationship**. Superficial relationships achieve very little in mentoring. Good mentoring involves bonding, connectedness, rapport, mateship, affinity, things in common and genuine concern. This will probably be best seen in peer mentoring but must be clearly evident in other forms of mentoring.
- **Dynamic.** The relationship should grow to be stimulating, empowering, flexible – very much alive. If and when it becomes passive, dull, stagnant, lifeless or rigid, it is time to terminate.
- **Intentional.** Meetings together will be purposeful and will have a clear sense of direction and expectation. Good preparation by the mentor, the setting of goals together, completion of assignments by the mentoree and prior consideration of the help needed, will keep the experience from becoming aimless or haphazard.
- **Trust.** A sense of trust usually takes time to develop. Growing confidence in each other results in increasing openness and honesty. The mentor's confidentiality, competence, credibility, wisdom, reliability, acceptance, exercise of basic skills such as

active listening, affirmation, encouragement and Christ-centredness all help deepen the levels of trust and develop strong bonding.

- **Enables.** Enabling means to make able, to assist, to work alongside; to provide the resources, the support, the stimulus for a person to be dynamically involved in the learning process rather than being a passive listener. The imagery here is more of a busy workshop with a variety of equipment and resources, with skilled supervisors and consultants facilitating the hands-on work of apprentices, rather than that of a 'teller' in a lecture theatre. Effective mentors are questioners, listeners and advisers rather than 'tellers'. Sessions together will be more inductive than didactic. Experience-based learning is foundational to mentoring. Therefore, mentors enable their mentorees to reflect on their life experiences.

- **Maximise the grace of God.** One of the prime roles of disciplemakers is that of helping another to be expectantly open to all the grace God has to offer them each day and in every situation. Maximising God's grace is anything but passive Christianity. It is about a most rigorous and comprehensive seeking after and receptivity to God's undeserved kindness, so as to deepen our relationship with him, to transform, to equip and to empower. Christ's Beatitude sums it up well, 'Blessed are those who hunger and thirst after righteousness [with the urgency and high motivation of a person ravenously hungry] for they will be filled' (Matt 5:6).

- **Mentoring** or coaching can easily focus too much on what a person says or does, to the neglect of their being. Equipping is about far more than skill development or the increase in knowledge and understanding of Christian resources. A mentoree's personal and spiritual life must receive constant review, for here lies the secret to success, from God's perspective. The purpose of maximising God's grace is primarily so that life becomes a series of new beginnings; each day is a new Easter, a resurrection to a fuller experience of living and loving like Christ.

- **Service.** Christian mentoring also concerns itself with making the most of God's grace by helping another recognise and respond to God's call to serve him through the gifts, fruits and graces imparted for ministry by the Holy Spirit. Paul encourages Timothy not only to enable others to serve, but to raise up leaders. 'And the things you have heard from me . . . entrust to faithful people who will be able to teach others as well' (2 Tim 2:2).

OTHER DEFINITIONS

Gunter Krallmann gives this definition: 'A mentor in the biblical sense establishes a close relationship with a protégé and on that basis through fellowship, modelling, advice, encouragement, correction, practical assistance and prayer support influences his/her understudy to gain a deeper comprehension of divine truth, lead a godlier life and render more effective service to God.'[1]

J Robert Clinton defines mentoring of potential leaders: 'Mentoring refers to the process in which a person with a serving, giving, encouraging attitude (Mentor), sees the leadership potential in a still to be developed person and is able to prompt or otherwise significantly influence that person along to the realisation of his/her potential.'[2]

Bishop John Reid takes Jesus' words to Peter as the basis for a biblical definition: 'Peter was commissioned by Jesus to strengthen his other followers, "*. . . help your brothers be stronger . . .*" (Luke 22:32). Just as Jesus enabled him to minister, Peter was to do the same with his peers. Mentoring describes an intentional and deliberate attitude to encourage another's life and ministry. It finds its biblical base in Jesus' words to Peter.'

—✳✳✳—

MENTORING – PART OF THE FABRIC OF LIFE

Increasingly, those who take their Christian discipleship and service seriously are seeing the value of having a friend and adviser with whom they can share openly and to whom they can be accountable. As the wise old sage said, 'Two are better than one' (Eccl 4:9).

Mentoring has always been part of the fabric of society. Parents play a major role in mentoring their children, especially in their earlier years. The artisan/apprentice relationship or the coach of an individual sportsperson or team are common forms of mentoring or coaching. There is a growing emphasis upon mentoring at all levels of commerce, industry, education and public life. An abundance of secular training courses and resources on the subject are widely promoted.

Mentoring was a way of life in Bible times. A few of the more prominent mentoring relationships were Jethro and Moses; Moses and Joshua; David and Jonathan; Barnabas and Paul; Lois and Eunice with Timothy; Priscilla and Aquila with Apollos, and Paul and Timothy. Jesus, with his disciples, provides our prime mentoring model.

The New Testament is full of 'one another' and 'together' passages pointing to Christianity as relational, about community, the power of togetherness. Rugged individualism and do-it-yourself spirituality are contrary to New Testament spirituality.

John Wesley's 'General Rules for Methodist Fellowships' (Societies) released in 1743 included, 'Watch over one another in love'. This was the key to his success in retaining those who were converted through that revival. In class meetings and one-to-one, they cared for one another.

Although mentoring or disciplemaking has always been practised in the church to varying degrees, in more recent years there has been a renewed emphasis. There are a growing number of books and seminars addressing the subject.

—✳✳✳—

MENTORING IN PERSPECTIVE

The following diagram draws together some of the main aspects of mentoring which will be dealt with in this book.

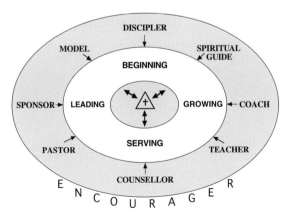

At the centre is a triangle emphasising that at the **heart** of Christian mentoring is **God, the Father, the Son and the Holy Spirit**. The first section of Chapter 2 seeks to underscore this by explaining the words 'into the name of the Father, the Son and the Holy Spirit' in Christ's great commission.

The cross in the triangle reminds us that all the grace of God we need for each day is readily available through what Christ accomplished by his life, death and resurrection. The cross is central to the diagram because Christ called us to follow him, to love as he loved, to live and work as he did. The New Testament writers are continually calling us to **Christ-centred living**.

The double-ended arrows point to both a **receiving** and a **giving** in our relationship to God. Receiving his grace in Christ in response to his invitation in Christ is balanced by giving our thanksgiving, our love and our renewed commitment in regular worship.

The next area illustrates the Christian life as a process of **becoming**. It has a beginning – in different ways, but always as an act of faith in Christ's finished work of redemption. The call of all the New Testament is to keep growing in Christ – to press on to spiritual maturity.

Servanthood is the outward working of the inner work of faith for the authentic follower of Christ. Christ is our supreme example. Every disciple is indwelt by the Holy Spirit and therefore gifted and empowered to serve. We will lead in various ways to bless others. In gratitude and love, like Isaiah, we say 'Here am I – send me!'

The **equipping** of leaders is one of our prime tasks and is never-ending. Indeed, this is one of the main keys to growing the Kingdom of God.

This takes us to the outer area of mentoring, which has as its aim the facilitation of this process. In doing so, we will exercise different roles. The roles shown here are explained in detail later. Mentors need to be flexible and use the role which is most appropriate to the changing needs of their mentorees.

Permeating all our mentoring will be a spirit of **encouragement**. We will affirm every sincere effort to bring pleasure to God and we will celebrate wins. Even when we have to be firm, it will be with grace so that our mentorees are always left with hope.

The secret of success essentially lies in the empowerment of God the Holy Spirit. Christian mentoring is all about making disciples and leaders under the direction and enabling of the Spirit of God, so that Jesus Christ may be praised.

—※※※—

It Works!

Those involved in different aspects of mentoring testify to its effectiveness.

Being a Mentor

'I can't think of many greater privileges than being asked to be a mentor to a fellow traveller. It is a position of honour, because that person is expressing trust and confidence in me – not only that I might have something to contribute, but also that I am someone with whom they wish to explore the endless horizons of God's grace. I don't presume to know God's will for them. But it is a privilege to listen carefully to their joys and sorrows, to encourage and support them, to pray with them and for them, and to keep pointing them to Jesus as their reason for living, loving and serving. Yes, it costs me time. But since time is precious to me, it is a special gift that I give, freely and with love. Yes, I must put aside my own concerns and focus on the needs of the one I mentor. But since I can sometimes spend too much time worrying about me, it is a special gift that the mentoree gives me in enabling me to give myself in their service. And in the whole process, I find that God has much to say to me, and that I too am enriched and encouraged.'

Mentoring Each Other

'As friends, we strive to be a living embodiment of our ever-present Lord to each other – always available, passionately encouraging, attentively listening and unconditionally loving. Talking openly about our joys and struggles, showing mutual respect and praying together grows us together. Often we find ourselves with more questions than answers to the issues with which we struggle. At times there are disappointments and frustrations with each other, but our commitment is such that we persevere. We hold each other to the issues of life the Scriptures are about, finding that accountability is a subset of good friendships. Two are certainly better than one!'

HAVING A MENTOR

'The phone rings at home. My 9-year-old daughter answers and talks for a few minutes. She hands the phone to me, "Daddy, it's for you." My mentor says, "G'day. I was praying for you this morning and thought I'd call to see how you are. Let me share with you what I was reading in the Bible this morning . . ." The impact of these calls on my family is huge. My mentor takes time and shows a prayerful interest not just in my ministry but my family. He has time to speak with my daughter, sons and wife – whoever gets to the phone first. He cares for and takes a genuine interest in them. All the more impressive when I realise this is a busy, older man who prays for me and then calls.

'I face a new issue in ministry to phone my mentor. He listens to the issue, offers advice and prayer. A few days later he calls back to inquire about the outcome.

'When we meet face-to-face, he asks questions of my relationship with Jesus, with my wife, children and church. While held accountable, there is no condemnation – only the encouragement to keep serving in a way that honours Christ.

'All in all, the privilege of having a mentor is to know I do not run alone. Someone is barracking for me. I know someone who is further down the track beckoning, calling, encouraging, pointing out pitfalls, pointing to Christ so I might run a better race. That's the joy of not running alone.'

✳✳✳

YOU CAN DO IT!

The Australian tennis player John Newcombe has said that encouragement is what makes champions. He said that while ability and skill is important, if there is no sense of being encouraged, then it is hard to go on.

How often have you encouraged another person? Perhaps it was a member of your family or a friend, someone in your workplace, a neighbour, or a person at your church. At that moment you were mentoring!

- *'I have discovered I often function informally as a mentor without realising it. I now have some clues on how to function better.'*
- *'I find I have been mentoring for a long time, but didn't know what it was called – good to know it has a name!'*

These are typical of comments frequently made by participants in my Mentoring Seminars.

The fact that you are reading this book suggests that you are already mentoring, whether you are aware of it or not. If you have some meaningful relationships in place, you are no doubt listening carefully and caring about others.

> **Mentoring is a very significant role every Christian disciple can fulfil . . . irrespective of age or experience. It is not restricted to 'giants of the faith'. The basic requirement is a living relationship with God and an ability to listen and respond sensitively, and to encourage. If this is true of you, you can be God's agent in enriching another person's life.**

In *Men Are from Mars, Women Are from Venus*, John Gray says, 'When a Martian gets upset he never talks about what is bothering him. He would never burden another Martian with his problem unless his friend's assistance was necessary to solve the problem . . . If he can't find a solution then he does something to forget his problems, like reading the news or playing a game . . . On Venus, sharing your problems with another actually is considered a sign of love and trust, not a burden. Venusians are not ashamed of having problems. Their egos are dependent not on looking "competent" but rather on being in loving relationships. They openly share feelings of being overwhelmed, confused, hopeless and exhausted.

'A Venusian feels good about herself when she has loving friends with whom to share her feelings and problems. A Martian feels good when he can solve his problems on his own in his cave. These secrets of feeling good are still applicable today.'

From an early age, our Western society applauds and reinforces the qualities of confidence, independence and self-reliance in **men**. While men are competent at mentoring and being mentored in the workplace, many find it difficult to take a peer into their confidence regarding their personal life. They fear to share their inner struggles, thoughts and feelings, lest the very act of disclosure erodes others' confidence in them, leaving them vulnerable and isolated.

Women are natural mentors and co-mentors. Peer mentoring usually happens more easily for them if they make friendships more intentional by helping one another think through their problems rather than merely supporting each other.

I have found many mature, godly women baulk at mentoring because they say they don't wish to give the impression of being superior to others. The New Testament affirms the role of women in mentoring. Eunice and Lois, Timothy's mother and grandmother, mentored him from an early age until he became a mentoree of Paul. Priscilla is always mentioned in the New Testament with her husband Aquila, as ministering together, assisting Paul and mentoring Apollos at Ephesus, enabling him to become one of the most powerful spokespersons for the Christian gospel.

Some of the best mentoring is done by very **busy people** who are disciplined with the use of their time.

Many who are **housebound** because of young families or physical disability mentor effectively by means of their phones or by inviting others to visit them.

Mentoring is a fulfilling role for **seniors** who may have fewer time restraints than previously. A very active friend who 'retired' from parish ministry ten years ago writes a letter of encouragement each day, especially to leaders, and regularly mentors many face to face.

As a senior, I find mentoring emerging leaders one of the most satisfying aspects of what has been a very diverse and fulfilling ministry. I'm inspired by the idealism, enthusiasm and responsiveness of the emerging leaders with whom I work. They rejuvenate me! I find great joy in seeing them grow. Like Caleb, who was still fired up at 85 ('Give me this mountain . . .'), many seniors who mentor regularly are growing older as participants rather than spectators!

YOU CAN DO IT – this book tells you how!

---

[1] *Mentoring for Mission*, Gunter Krallmann, Jensco Hong Kong & Globe Europe, 1992

[2] *Connecting*, Paul D Stanley, J Robert Clinton, Navpress, 1992

CHAPTER 2

SOME BIBLICAL FOUNDATIONS

CHRISTIAN MENTORING AS DISCIPLEMAKING

As has been explained earlier, the root of the word for mentoring can be traced back to Greek mythology. It is now extensively used in both church and community organisations to describe the one-to-one nurture of individuals in their life and work. Many words are used in the New Testament which relate to this task of nurturing. These are often found in the 'one another' or 'together' passages (loving, caring for, watching over, bearing burdens, encouraging, praying, exhorting, rebuking, spurring on, etc. The tasks of pastoring, teaching, oversight, etc all relate to the support of followers of Christ in their personal and spiritual growth and equipping for ministry.

In what has become known as Christ's great commission in Matthew 28:19,20, he gives his disciples clear goals to pursue in order to continue his ministry of building the Kingdom of God.

'All authority in heaven and on earth has been given to me. Go therefore and make disciples of all nations, baptising them in the name of the Father and of the Son and of the Holy Spirit, and teaching them to obey everything that I have commanded you. And remember, I am with you always, to the end of the age.'

'Disciple' is a favourite word of Matthew's. He uses it 73 times in his gospel. It refers to any person, male or female, who is rightly related to Jesus Christ. Disciples in this gospel are those who follow Christ, are committed to him and his teachings. They call him 'Lord' because they own him as their master, their king and their God, and seek to live in obedience to him. Those who are not

17

his followers in this gospel record refer to him as 'teacher' – someone to be listened to, to debate with, maybe to learn from or to be impressed by, but not to be committed to.

'Disciple' literally means learner. Christian disciples take Jesus Christ the Son of God as their teacher and model.

Luke in his parallel account of Christ's commissioning of his followers, records Jesus calling them forth to be his witnesses. 'You are witnesses of these things' (Luke 24:48). A witness is someone who gives evidence of what they observe personally, not a carried story or hearsay, but a testimony to a personal experience. Previously Jesus has said 'these things' are his suffering, death and resurrection that are to be preached to all to call them to repentance and forgiveness (vv 46,47). In Acts, Luke showed what tremendous witnesses they became after being empowered by the Holy Spirit. They so faithfully testified to 'these things'. In the first few chapters, Luke refers to them as witnesses seven times. The two words 'disciple' and 'witness' give a good balance.

We don't 'try hard' to understand and practise Jesus' teaching and emulate his peerless example in our own strength. The ability to do this stems from an intimate personal relationship with him – a personal experience of all the grace that is made available through his death and resurrection. That relationship and the capacity to faithfully witness to Christ is made possible by the empowerment of the Holy Spirit whom Jesus revealed would himself be the prime witness to him (John 15:26,27).

So this is the grace relationship with Christ that we should endeavour to help our mentorees develop: that of disciples and witnesses to him.

'Make disciples': The key verb here is 'make disciples' – the other 'doing words' are subordinate to it. They instruct in how this is to be achieved – the means, the methods. 'Go', 'baptising', 'teaching' summarise what is involved in bringing people to faith in Christ, nurturing their growth and equipping them as participants in Christ's continuing ministry – disciplemaking. Making disciples is the text for mentors. Unfortunately the word 'making' has 'enforcer' connotations. The reality is that the mentor is the Christ-like leader who is commissioned to make Christ-like disciples. It needs to be emphasised that the mentor is an enabler who facilitates credible discipleship through Christ, rather than being the self-sufficient professional builder. God is the mentor. Christian mentors are under-mentors.

Let us think about these other verbs or 'doing words' in relation to our purpose here.

'Go': Disciplemaking is anything but a passive task. It is dynamic. It is not about waiting for others to come to us (like the 'all welcome' bottom line on many church notice boards!). Christ instructs us to make a move, to take the initiative, to reach out. Some of those I mentor contacted me first, to ask if I could help them, but the majority responded after I felt drawn to them and quite deliberately said, 'If ever you think I can help in any way, don't hesitate to contact me.' Such an invitation leaves the door ajar to them if and when they think I can be of assistance. Sometimes I invite a person who has been on my mind to have coffee or a meal with me without stating my purpose, waiting to see what emerges.

In mentoring/disciplemaking, don't be backward. Act when you think the Spirit is prompting. Don't procrastinate – make a move, take the initiative, go! But do it gently and with sensitivity.

This part of Christ's great commission can also read 'as you go', implying 'in the routines of daily life', 'in our daily encounters'. Christ calls us to make disciples as a way of life, not in addition to the many other things we do. What a practical, non-threatening, manageable approach to mentoring, especially with those to whom we relate on a regular basis!

'Baptising': The appropriation of all that is symbolised in baptism, making it our own in everyday living, is an ongoing experience which is never complete in this life. So the word **'in'** in Christ's commission or perhaps better **'into'**, has a profound meaning. So much needless controversy has surrounded the symbolism and ritual of baptism that often this main aspect of a direct relationship to God takes a lesser place.

Basically, the idea of being baptised into the name of someone means to give one's allegiance to that person, to commit oneself to follow their leadership, to learn from them and to honour them (cf 1 Cor 10:2). Even more important is what God does for believers through baptism. God gives grace and new life and incorporates them into Christ's body.

Being baptised into the name of the Father focuses on God's sovereignty and his unconditional love and mercy.

Baptism into the name of the Son declares the supreme revelation of God's nature and undeserved love and kindness in all that Christ accomplished for us by his death – forgiveness of sins, cleansing through his shed blood and reconciling our lives to God (Rom 5:10; 1 Pet 1:18-21; 2 Cor 5:18 and 1 John 1:9). It is a symbolic public act that declares that a person is participating by faith in Christ's death and resurrection and openly identifying with the kingdom of God with Christ as Lord. Romans 6:1–11 and 13:11-14 are significant for us here.

It also proclaims his resurrection as the ultimate proof of Christ's divinity (Rom 1:4) and the seal upon all he did on the cross – his conquest of the power of sin and death and our sharing in his resurrection, victory and life (John 14:19; Rom 6:1-11; 1 Cor 15:12-22). It symbolises the dying to, and burial of, our self-centredness, 'putting aside deeds of darkness' (Rom 13:12), rising again to the new environment of the spiritual realm to a new way of living, a new empowerment (Phil 3:10) and responsible membership in the kingdom community – 'clothing ourselves with the Lord Jesus Christ' (Rom 13:14).

Baptism into the name of the Holy Spirit gathers up all that the New Testament teaches about the role of the Holy Spirit as the one who makes us like Christ (Rom 8:2-4,11; 1 Cor 1:30, 3:16; 1 Pet 1:2), reveals God and his will (1 Cor 2:12; Eph 2:8, 3:5), guides (Acts 1:8; 2:4; 8:29; 16:6,7; Rom 8:14; Gal 5:18), transforms (John 3:3,6; 1 Cor:12:13; Rom 8:9,16; 1 Cor 12:3; Titus 3:5; 1 John 5:1) and prays for us (Rom 8:26,27; Eph 6:18).

Baptism affirms that when a person receives Christ, the Holy Spirit begins a new work of grace. Each day one must be open to all the grace God has to give through the work of the Holy Spirit.

We need to note here that **'name'**, not 'names' is used by Christ. God is one – three Persons living in magnificent unity. Here is the ultimate in community, the zenith of relationships. Here is the crown of love – its purest expression. And, wonder of wonders, Jesus prayed to the Father that all his followers '. . . may be **in us**'. The gospel invites people to enter into a living relationship and community of love with God and therefore with each other (John 17:20-23).

There is no aspect of disciplemaking (Christian mentoring) from the New Testament perspective that does not include seeking to enable this crucial aspect of God-centred Christian living to occur. While in my mentoring I deal with many practical issues of life and ministry, what I seek to keep foremost is the need to maintain a close relationship with God as Father, Son and Holy Spirit.

'Teaching them . . .': In Chapter 5, I deal with how adults learn. The learning process in a mentor/mentoree relationship is guided by the adult learning principles of voluntary participation, mutual respect, collaborative spirit, action and reflection, critical reflection and self-direction.

Mentoring is not a dependable process but a facilitation of self-understanding and insight through reflection. Hopefully the outcome will finish up with a mentoree who is able to integrate his/her Christian faith, theology, inner-self with journey and ministry. Finishing up with an integrated and reflective person is the ideal outcome from this process.

Christian education emphasises not only the knowledge and understanding and teaching skills of the teacher, but the **modelling** of what is taught – a living demonstration of the gospel, albeit an imperfect one. We significantly enrich the learning process **by who we are** (our attitudes, our values, our behaviour), by **what we say** (and the conviction, the commitment and the illustrations from personal experience of the truth we seek to communicate) and what we do (our modelling, our example).

Content and method must be appropriate to the stage of maturity of the learner. This is recognised by the New Testament writers when they distinguish between the 'milk' and 'meat' of the Word to avoid giving indigestion to the immature and undernourishing the more developed.

'Teaching them to obey everything I have commanded you': Helping another to learn is integral to most if not all of the roles of a mentor. It is therefore important that as disciplemakers we understand what we are to help others to learn and how to do this most effectively.

Jesus clearly enunciates the core of the body of truth on which we are to focus – 'everything I have commanded you'. Much of

Christ's teaching is disturbing – Jesus was a radical! If Christ is taken seriously, it will result in costly discipleship. In our mentoring we will seek to help Christ's followers to walk in his steps (1 Pet 2:21), to take seriously **'everything'** he 'commanded'.

Christ's commission includes, 'teaching them to **obey** . . .' James warns against not taking seriously what is learnt (James 1:22-25). Intentionality, perseverance, **application** to life and action are all strongly encouraged – owning what we learn and its practical outworking in everyday living. Jesus likens the person who builds on a rock foundation to one who 'hears my words and puts them into practice' (Luke 6:46-49 – see also Luke 8:21; 11:28 and John 14:21).

Book stores are full of books on what to include in nurturing Christians. I wonder what would happen if, instead of using this material, we and our mentorees agreed to read one whole gospel in a few sittings between our meetings, praying that the Spirit address us, then sharing with each other what got our attention and its implications for our lives and ministries. After doing this with the gospels, maybe we could read sections of Jesus' teachings in a 'red-letter' edition in a similar way, beginning with the Beatitudes in Matthew's gospel.

While not wanting to deny our rich tradition of biblical knowledge (all the Bible helps, the commentaries and much more), we need to take another look at what Jesus taught about the role of the Holy Spirit in unlocking his teachings. John records Jesus saying, 'But the Counsellor, the Holy Spirit, whom the Father will send in my name, will **teach** you all things and remind you of everything I have said to you' (John 14:26). 'When he, the Spirit of truth, comes, he will **guide** you into all truth . . . taking from what is mine and making it known to you' (John 16:13,14). See also how this is applied in the epistle of John (1 John 2:20,27).

Our faithful leadership should aim to produce those who can lead others. One of the best texts on mentoring is 2 Tim 2:2, 'And the things you have heard me say in the presence of many witnesses entrust to reliable people who are qualified to teach others also.' The Greek word for 'also' is an ongoing verb. This means when we teach others, we teach those who are able to teach others, who are able to teach others, who are able to teach others, and so it goes on. This means the carbon copy method. Oops! The digital copy is as clear as the original. It is a powerful metaphor for mentoring and should actually make mentors hesitate before they undertake such a task. It is quite awesome that the mentor as Christ's representative makes disciples who are able to make disciples to teach others also! Producing a Christ-like disciple who 'can teach others also' is a formidable task.

The context of this 'great commission' can encourage us when we feel hesitant. Matthew 28:17 records that 'when they saw him . . . some **doubted**'. The Greek word translated 'doubted' here can also be translated 'living in suspense' or 'hesitated'. Theirs was not a total disbelief but a sort of hesitant response.

We too may hesitate in taking initiatives in mentoring, not because of doubts about Jesus but about ourselves. Both the words that precede Christ's commission and those that follow are most significant here. For some, the conviction that this was really the Jesus they knew previously came slowly – it was too good to be true! Before he gave these clear instructions to the eleven, he reminded them of his power of which they had seen glimpses in the miracles he performed. Now he declares his absolute authority over the whole universe, not just over storms, varied sicknesses, the earth's produce, the animal kingdom and death itself.

In the light of this, the words that follow Jesus' commission take on an even greater significance. Here is the remarkable **promise** of the One who is Lord of Creation – 'And surely **I am with you always**'. Those who first heard this call and promise were a most unlikely group – none would have seemed worthy of mention in the pages of history. But Christ's unfailing presence and power transformed them – and they set about changing the world.

In this book I use the words 'mentoring' and disciplemaking' synonymously because of the popular use of the word 'mentoring' both in the church and community. Even with its rich origins and contemporary usage, the expression **mentoring**, in the light of what we have considered here, is a poor second to the word **disciplemaking** in the Christian context. Our spiritual guidance, coaching, counselling, teaching, sponsoring, pastoring, resourcing, modelling, encouraging, all take on a deeper, richer, Christ-oriented dimension when we operate out of this biblical framework. God, the Father, the Son and the Holy Spirit, is our richest resource for Christian mentoring – disciplemaking.

Does this seem to place undue emphasis upon spirituality to the neglect of equipping for ministry – gifts, ministry skills, effective leadership strategies and a host more? From my observations I argue that so much coaching of leaders has been driven by secular management know-how (helpful though it may be) rather than by primarily trying to learn how Jesus related to his Father and went about his ministry.

Despite the yawning chasm between our contemporary culture and that of the first century and earlier, there are non-negotiable, eternal principles that are meant to guide Christian disciples and leaders. They must be our guideposts in every age for this sacred task.

In Matthew 11:28, Jesus issues his alluring invitation:

'Are you tired? Worn out? Burned out on religion?
Come to me. Get away with me and you'll recover your life.
I'll show you how to take a real rest.
WALK WITH ME and WORK WITH ME – WATCH HOW
I DO IT.
Learn the unforced rhythms of grace. I won't lay anything
heavy or ill-fitting on you.
KEEP COMPANY WITH ME and you'll learn to live freely
and lightly'.[1]

THAT'S IT! Mentoring/disciplemaking is meant to be a journey like the one we see on the road to Emmaus – two disciples in company with Jesus, **listening** intently, **watching** attentively. Then, hopefully we too, together with our mentorees, will 'feel on fire'!

STUDY GUIDE

PERSONAL REFLECTION

1. What encouragement do you receive from the symbolism of baptism presented here? How true has this been in your own experience?

2. 'Teaching them to obey everything I have commanded you.'
    • What aspects of Jesus' teaching do you find difficult or disturbing?

3. 'Read one whole gospel in a few sittings.'
   - Why not take up this challenge! (Then note any new perspectives on Jesus, and the feelings these engender.)
4. How has your Christian life and service been enriched by the example (modelling) of others?
5. How important do you think 'modelling' is in mentoring?
   - Why?
   - Are there aspects of your own life where you need to seek more grace to be a better model?
     What do you need to do?
6. In what ways were the first and last sentences of Christ's commission ('All authority. . .' and '. . .I am with you. . .') significant to his disciples, faced with the daunting task he gave them?
   - How significant are they for you in serving him?

GROUP WORK
1. Share any of your individual work, taking one section at a time on the topics you each wish to share.
2. In what ways does the word 'disciplemaking' give greater significance to this ministry?

—✻✻✻—

AN ADEQUATE IDEA OF GOD

The foundation of all Christian mentoring is who God has revealed himself to be. We can easily be tricked into thinking God is less than he is. Success in mentoring is to a large extent dependent upon the mentor's own knowledge, understanding and personal experience of God as revealed primarily in Scripture. This will undergird all she/he does in equipping the mentoree.

In this training, frequent mention is made of the linking of mentorees with the resources they need for their life and service. The **primary** resource of both the mentor and the mentoree is **God**. The mentor will frequently remind the person they are helping of the all-sufficiency of God, and encourage faith in him. Other aspects of God's nature will need to be recalled at appropriate times.

Most of the **problems** we face from time to time grow out of an **inadequate idea of God**. It is all too easy to have a lopsided view of God. Our focus can be upon his power and might to the neglect of his gentleness and kindness. Our concentration on his loving closeness can outweigh his holiness and severity with all that spoils his creatures and creation.

God's revelation of himself in Scripture presents a robust, strong, healthy understanding of who he really is. The Bible introduces us to **God** who **is adequate** – sufficient for all our needs and therefore deserving of our trust, our love and our worship. 'With God, all things are possible' (Matt 19:26), taught Jesus. Paul wrote, 'My God will meet all your needs according to his glorious riches in Christ Jesus' (Phil 4:19).

The faith, hope and love we all need to live and serve Christ in a way that will bring praise to him, and build the kingdom of God, grow out of this big picture of God.

> 'But this I call to mind,
> and therefore I have hope:
> The steadfast love of the Lord never ceases,
> his mercies never come to an end;
> They are new every morning;
> great is your faithfulness.
> "The Lord is my portion," says my soul,
> "therefore I will hope in him." '
>
> (Lam 3:21-24)

GOD IS UNCONDITIONAL LOVE

God is love. He is the source of all true love. God doesn't have moods, doesn't get tired and doesn't get sick. His love is unchanging, always the same, always reaching out – it 'never ceases'.

The supreme demonstration of his love is seen in Christ's death to redeem us and set us free. We can't earn it, it is always undeserved – a gift for the receiving. (1 John 4:8-16; Rom 5:8; John 3:16; Deut 33:3; Isa 63:9; Eph 2:4; 1 John 3:1).

GOD IS MERCIFUL, FULL OF GRACE

'Grace' means undeserved kindness. God is undeservedly kind. There is no limit to his kindness, 'his mercies never, never come to

26

an end' (Eccl 3:22). His mercy, his kindness, is not on the market. It cannot be earned. It is a free gift, available to all (Ps 103:8-18; 145:8,9; Zeph 3:17; Rom 2:4).

GOD IS FAITHFUL

God is utterly trustworthy. He never lets us down. He doesn't get too busy, or sidetracked, hasn't got a bad memory, his patience doesn't wear thin. He is always there for us, just when and how we need him. You can stake everything on God – he will never, never let you down (Gen 28:15; Ps 36:5; 111:7-9; Isa 44:21; Jer 33:14; Lam 3:22,23; 1 Cor 10:13; Heb 10:23; 1 John 1:9).

GOD IS HOLY AND RIGHTEOUS

God is separated from all that is impure, evil and untrue. It is his nature to be righteous – it is impossible for him to act otherwise. He is goodness, truth and beauty. He is just and exercises judgment on all who seek to pervert or destroy the glorious ideal he has for all of his creation, which is to reflect his nature (Ezra 9:15; Ps 11:7, 22:3; 99:5,9; 103:6; Isa 1:4, 6:1-3 etc; John 17:11, 25; Rom 2:2, 3:4-6; 1 Pet 1:15,16).

GOD IS EVER-PRESENT

He is actively engaged in every part of his creation. There is no place or circumstance in which we find ourselves where God is not present. We never walk alone. He is always there, always present. God is always with us (Ps 139:7-19; Jer 23:24; Acts 17:24-28; Isa 66:1).

GOD IS ALL-KNOWING

God's knowledge is absolute. He knows everything. He knows what happened to us in the past, what is happening to us at this moment, and what will happen to us in the future (Ps 33:13-15; 139:1-6; Ezek 11:5; Amos 9:1-4; Acts 15:18; 1 John 3:20).

GOD IS ALL-POWERFUL

God is Lord of all. He is sovereign of time and space, and of eternity. His power is always creative. He never acts contrary to his nature. He normally works in his creation in 'ordinary' ways (which we call 'natural laws') but sometimes he works in 'extraordinary' ways (which we call miracles). 'With God all things are possible' (Matt 19:26, also Job 42:2; Ps 95:3, 135:6; Jer 32:17; Mark 14:36; Luke 1:37).

GOD IS **THE MENTOR**

God takes the initiative in all ministry in his name. Therefore effective ministry involves making ourselves available to him to be guided to where he is already at work. Then we are but the channels through whom he works.

God is endlessly at work in the world through the Holy Spirit. The function of God the Holy Spirit is to extend the work of Christ (John 16:7). The Holy Spirit is 'the Lord and life-giver . . .' (Nicene Creed). He is the one who transforms human lives. He is God with us, transcendent and also immanent, in such a way as to make a reality in the life and witness of the true Christian disciple, all the grace God offers us in Christ. The Holy Spirit equips and empowers us for ministry (Eph 3:16; 1 Cor 2:4; Rom 15:13; Acts 1:8, 4:31).

In seeking to identify our possible mentoring relationships, the above gives us confidence that God has already prepared the way – he has already taken the initiative (Deut 31:8). As we take time to reflect on our framework of relationship, we will get 'hunches' about whom to approach.

God is our prime mentor. But God does not only plan for our mentoring needs in terms of others to be mentored by or to mentor. All human relationships will be secondary to the development and maintenance of our growing relationship to God as we practise the spiritual disciplines of prayer, obedience to the Scriptures, solitude, worship, service, fellowship, etc.

The **openness** and **honesty** we will need to make effective mentoring relationships grows out of our openness with and obedience to God.

From this living relationship will come our **empowerment** by the Holy Spirit to mentor others.

28

STUDY GUIDE

PERSONAL REFLECTION

1. When have you felt most loved by God, by his people?

2. Why do you think the writer of Lamentations, writing in a situation of desolation and utter despair for his nation, found hope in the characteristics of God that he introduces in Lamentations 3:21-23?
    • Is there a word of encouragement to you here regarding a situation you are facing?

3. Think of some situations in which you could be an 'apostle of hope'. What would it involve? (Remember, being hopeful involves facing reality, not avoiding it!)

4. Select one of the above aspects of God's nature which is especially relevant to your own present situation. In what ways would you be different if you took this characteristic of God seriously?

5. Is there someone you are trying to help, for whom one of the above is especially relevant? How do you think it could help?

6. Can you see any significance in the order in which the characteristics of God are listed above – that the list commences with God being unconditional love and ends with God as all-powerful, rather than the reverse?

GROUP WORK

1. Share as much as you wish of your individual work.

2. What are the practical implications for our mentoring when we accept that 'God is the mentor'?

3. In his letter to the Romans, Paul encourages his readers to balance God's kindness (grace) with his sternness (severity) (Rom 11:22). What are some of the consequences of over-emphasising one to the neglect of the other?

—✳✳✳—

HAVING A SANE ESTIMATE OF OURSELVES AND OTHERS

Our mentoring will be greatly hindered if we have an immature or sub-Christian concept of self. The problems we have in understanding ourselves distort the way we relate to others. An adequate self-esteem provides a sound basis for our ministry to others.

The Scriptures teach us to avoid having too great an opinion of ourselves – putting too high a valuation on who we are and on our performance – as it leads to self-conceit and censure of those who differ from us. Jesus spoke strongly of the Pharisees in this regard (Matt 23:6,8) and encouraged his disciples to pursue servanthood and humility (Matt 23:11). Pride is always strongly censured (Deut 8:17; Jer 9:23; Prov 11:2, 16:18; Rom 12:16; 1 Cor 10:12, etc).

On the other hand, the Scriptures make it plain that we are not to despise ourselves. Paul wrote, 'Don't cherish exaggerated ideas of yourself and your own importance, but try to have a sane estimate of your capabilities by the light of the faith that God has given to us all' (Rom 12:3, J B Phillips).

The ego is God's creation and our selfhood is what will stand in the presence of God in eternity. This is the part of us with which God has fellowship. Jesus said as well as loving God wholeheartedly, we are to love our neighbour **as we love ourselves**. Christ-inspired love for ourselves is as necessary for our own wholeness and holiness as it is for our love for God and for other people. John Wesley wrote, 'Self-love is not a sin; it is an indisputable duty'.

In thinking our way to a sober estimate of ourselves, the Bible helps us gain a balanced perspective. It provides a firm foundation for a sound self-esteem and a greater appreciation of the worth and diversity among human beings. In the Scriptures, we are presented with God's perspective – people are perceived as image bearers, flawed and wounded.

Image Bearer: Men and women are people of dignity, 'created in the image of God', 'in God's likeness'! (Gen 1:26,27; 5:1). They are 'made a little lower than angels, crowned with glory and honour' (Ps 8:5; 21:5). Theologians have thought hard and long about what that really means, but whatever it means, it is mind-boggling! People are unique in God's creation, very special beings. They are made with a capacity to live in close fellowship with God. They are created to receive love from and to give love to God, and to be channels of God's love to others.

Flawed: Human beings have sinned; we have all 'fallen short of the glory of God', of God's glorious plan. We have 'forfeited the glory of God' (Rom 3:23). We are not what God intended us to be. Outside of Christ we are alienated from our holy and gracious, loving heavenly Father (Isa 59:2). Even born-again Christians are not without sin. But the incredible good news, the wonderful word of hope, is that life can begin again (2 Cor 5:17). Christ died and rose again to deal with sin and its consequences (Rom 5:1,2,6-8). Through repentance and faith (Acts 2:38) we can be 'transformed into his likeness' (2 Cor 3:18; Eph 4:24; Col 3:10; 1 John 3:1-3). There is hope! What a privilege to be called to experience this personally and then pass it on to all to whom we minister!

Wounded: All of us carry scars from hurts we have received from being members of a flawed community. Christ's gracious and loving invitation is to all 'who are weary and burdened', 'all who carry heavy loads'. To such he offers 'rest', and relief (Matt 11:28). We work with many people for whom life has lost its meaning (Eccl 6:12), broken people who know the real meaning of suffering and weakness. With empathy and sensitivity we point them graciously to the divine healer (2 Cor 12:7-10; Heb 4:15,16; 7:25).

> The vision God gives us in Christ is all about possibilities – what might be, not what is. People need not be locked into more of the same. It is about new realities which can be seen and apprehended by faith. The Good News is that life can begin again! God's call is to actualise through the Spirit what we already are in Christ – a new creation! (2 Cor 5:17)

In Christ – a Child of God: As mentors, we will frequently remind those we mentor of their privileged position through faith in Christ, and encourage them to live as a child of the King of kings, claiming the privileges and accepting the responsibilities.

Many passages in the New Testament give instruction on this topic. Here are just a few aspects of our status in Christ, drawn mainly from Paul's writings in Rom 8:13-17; Gal 3:26, 4:4-7; Eph 1:4-9 and Rev 21:7.

- Redeemed, forgiven, set free
- Adopted children of God
- Special rights as God's children
- Heirs of God
- Empowered by God's Spirit – who gives certainty, confidence, guidance
- Orientation to a new way of life
- New purpose for living – to bring praise to God

Each aspect of this scriptural perception of human beings applies to us as mentors as well as to those we seek to help. God sees every facet of us, the good as well as the bad, the potential for success as well as the failure, our alienation and the hope of restoration through his grace. He sees us as 'in process' rather than as a product. As becomers, learners, God's people, 'saints' in the making rather than people who have arrived. In seeking to be Christ's agents of change in ministering to others we often have to discard past conditioning, which results in blinkered vision, and seek to see ourselves and others as God sees us, and hold to that divine broad view.

There is the important aspect of **attitude** that we must also consider here, for our attitude determines our ministry. J B Phillips, who helped the New Testament come alive in new ways through his then fresh translation into contemporary English, suffered deep depression for most of his life. In a book written about him, he is described as a **wounded healer**. He was flooded with letters from needy people because of the positive impression that his paraphrases gave of him, as a person. Henri Nouwen used this description of Phillips as the title for one of his popular books. We minister out of the awareness of our unworthiness, our incompleteness and our weakness. But as Paul reminds us, God's grace is sufficient and it is in our deep sense of **weakness** that we find a strength that is divinely given (2 Cor 12:7-10). As D T Niles has it, we are beggars telling other beggars where to find food!

STUDY GUIDE

PERSONAL REFLECTION

1. Why do you think it is difficult for so many followers of Christ to have a 'sane estimate' of themselves, avoiding the extremes of pride and poor self-image?
   - How true is this of you?
   - What feelings does this evoke in you?
   - What practical steps could you take, with the help of God and others, to deal with what emerges for you here?

2. In what ways does this fourfold biblical perspective on human beings touch your personal experience?
   - How would you relate your present pain, confusion or uncertainty to this biblical teaching?
   - What word of hope is there for you here?

3. How could what is presented here make you more positive, understanding and/or hopeful in helping others. (You may want to relate it to a specific person without mentioning his/her name.)

4. Try to match the last section of the above ('In Christ – a Child of God') with the relevant Scripture passages.
   - Choose one or two and discuss what privileges and responsibilities are implied.

5. If God has got your attention in some matters through any of the above, what response could you make?
   - Who is there to help you?

GROUP WORK

1. Discuss 1 and 3 above.

2. Share your responses to 2 if you feel comfortable about doing so.

3. Discuss the statement 'The vision God gives us in Christ. . .' in relation to our mentoring roles.

—✳✳✳—

WALKING THE ROAD TOGETHER

Another foundation of Christian mentoring is the biblical teaching on fellowship with other Christians. Christianity is a **relational** religion. It is **not individualistic**. It is a fellowship of love, centred on Christ. The metaphors of 'vine', 'body', 'building' in the New Testament emphasise the idea of **community** and **interdependence**. The Greek word commonly rendered as 'fellowship' is koinonia, which literally means the state of sharing, of being partners, of having common or mutual interests. We are not meant to try to make it on our own, we need each other. In Ecclesiastes 4:9-12, the idea of partnership, of walking the road together, is clearly encouraged:

'. . . Two are better than one, because they have a good reward for their toil. For if they fall, one will lift up the other; but woe to the one who is alone and falls and does not have another to help. Again, if two lie together, they keep warm; but how can one keep warm alone? And though one might prevail against another, two will withstand one. A threefold cord is not quickly broken.'

'Iron sharpens iron and one person sharpens the wits of another' (Prov 27:17) further underscores the idea of keeping each other sharp or effective.

Moffatt describes a Christian wanting to live in isolation as a 'pious particle'. Howard Hendricks warns, 'A person trying to make it on their own is an accident waiting to happen'. Wesley said, 'The Bible knows nothing of solitary religion'. He instructed his followers '. . . to watch over one another in love . . .'

There are numerous 'one another' and 'together' passages in the New Testament. One of special relevance here is:

*'. . . let us consider how we may **spur one another** on toward love and good deeds. Let us not give up **meeting together**, as some are in the habit of doing, but let us **encourage one another** – and all the more as you see the Day approaching.'* (Heb 10:24,25)

The words **'spur on'** are very strong words. They imply calling forth, summonsing, inviting, prodding, urging, earnestly appealing to, inspiring to act.

Likewise, **'encourage'** is rich with meaning. It suggests supporting, assisting, inspiring, consoling, comforting, increasing hope and confidence, and urging on.

The Greek word for encourage comes from the same root as advocate, counsellor, comforter, the same word that is used in John's gospel for the Holy Spirit. We can therefore rightly make the link between the Holy Spirit's ministry as that of supporter, strengthener, helper, sponsor, advocate and our ministry of encouragement – his ministry through us (John 12-15; 14:16,17,26; 16:7,8; Rom 8:26; Eph 5:21-25; 2 Tim 1:14).

Accountability. Another aspect of the biblical teaching on mutual support often overlooked or rejected is accountability. This involves being open and honest with each other about our doubts, our fears, our failures, as well as our joys and successes – in other words, to be accountable. This is at the **heart** of all **effective mentoring**.

This commitment must also include the aims and purposes of all that makes up the mentoring experience – the way the relationship is maintained, the conduct of each session and work done in between times.

'The basis of accountability is the biblical teaching on **covenant**, which is a major theme in the Bible. It is a solemn agreement and promise, often made binding by an oath, and witnessed and guaranteed by God. Personal covenants were common in ancient Israel, eg between Jacob and Laban (Gen 31:44-55), Ruth and Naomi (Ruth 1:15-17), David and Jonathan (1 Sam 18:3). The divine covenant is also the most unifying single theme in Old Testament religion. God made a covenant with Noah (Gen 9:8-17), Abraham (Gen 15 and 17:1-14), Moses (Exod 19:24), and David (2 Sam 7:8-16).

The failure of Israel to live by these covenants led the prophets to speak of the emergence of 'a new covenant' (Jer 31:31-34) which would involve a new beginning, an intimate relationship with God, and would be internal rather than external. The New Testament represents Christians as living within this new covenant of grace, initiated by God, sealed by the blood of Jesus Christ, involving an intimate personal relationship with God, promising final redemption and eternal membership in the household of God, and imposing on us the **duty** to love one another as Christ loved us (John 13:34).

The **implications** for us are that as we stand within this covenant relationship with God we are united with all other Christian believers and therefore must **moderate our individualism**. Of special significance for us here is that our own covenants with one another stand within the context of the divine covenant and are to mirror it.'[2]

It is imperative that accountability be administered in a spirit of grace and not law. It must reflect the spirit of the divine covenant. While it is reasonable in a mentoring relationship to have high expectations of people who thoughtfully and prayerfully commit themselves to each other, we must avoid creating a legalistic spirit in the relationship. A lazy or undisciplined person will need to be nudged. A healthy mentoring relationship involves exhortation and rebuke, but this always must take place in an atmosphere of pastoral love and patience. Essentially, mentoring is about 'watching over one another in love'.

STUDY GUIDE

PERSONAL REFLECTION

1. What are the disadvantages of living 'as a pious particle', as Moffatt puts it?

2. Who are those with whom you share your life and ministry?
   • What does that mean for you?

3. In what ways do you need to be 'spurred on'?
   • Who could encourage and support you?

4. How do you feel when you are encouraged by someone? (Try to recall some recent experiences.)
   • When did you last encourage someone?
   • How did they respond?

5. What are the implications for you as a mentor of having your ministry so closely aligned with that of the Holy Spirit?

6. What do you feel moved to do now?

GROUP WORK

1. Share as much of the above as you wish. (Allow all who wish to share on the same point to do so, then move onto the next.)

2. What are the strengths and weaknesses of accountability?

BIBLICAL MENTORING MODELS
JESUS – OUR PRIME MODEL

Jesus provides our one and only truly perfect model, message and method to direct our mentoring under the guidance and empowerment of the Holy Spirit.

Mark tells us, 'He appointed twelve that they might be with him . . .' (Mark 3:14). He moulded the lives of his disciples by sharing the whole of his life with them. By his life, he demonstrated how to bring pleasure to God, how best to serve and honour him so that others might take God seriously and give him his rightful place in their lives.

We must learn how he went about being with his disciples, from their immature first steps to their becoming leaders who would be strong pillars of his kingdom, after their Pentecost experience.

He provides not only our best example but he is our own best mentor. To reflect to any worthwhile degree on the way he moulded the lives of the twelve, we also need to share his life.

However, it is vital to appreciate that there was one regular aspect of his life in which, until his Gethsemane, the disciples participated only indirectly. Those were his times of solitude with his Father when, before dawn and at least once, all night, he maintained that intimacy which undergirded and empowered his whole life and ministry (Mark 1:35; Luke 6:12-15). Here is probably the greatest lesson we must keep learning – to find and frequent our places of solitude, our desert place, our retreat, where as our Lord did, we can take unhurried time to keep God-centred.

HIS BEING: Probably what the disciples would remember best from being continually with Jesus was who he was as a person – his character, his integrity, his credibility, his uniqueness.

Growth of their characters was Jesus' primary concern. This took place essentially by observation and in close relationship with him as they participated in his simple lifestyle and his dynamic ministry (Matt 8:20). The disciples were continually exposed to his genuine compassion for the poor and the sick (Mark 1:41; Luke 7:13); the crowds with their varied needs (Matt 9:36); those with status (Mark 10:21) and any who rejected him (Matt 23:37). They were almost overcome with his servant leadership and great humility (Matt 9:10; Luke 22:27; John 13:5-17; 2 Cor 8:9; Phil 2:7,8); awed by his authority in his teaching (Matt 7:29) and power to perform miracles (Mark 1:23-26; Matt 8:23-27; Matt 9:18-26); and stunned with the vehemence of his righteous indignation at hypocrisy (Matt 23:1-26) and injustice (Mark 11:15-18).

They would have been impressed with his concern for the weak and marginalised. Little children had ready access to him (Mark 10:13-16) and a despised Samaritan, rather than religious Jews, was the 'good' man in his parable (Luke 10:25-37).

As mentors, what a challenge Jesus presents to us, to become like him. How important is our own credibility, our believability. But this is not something we generate entirely in our own strength. Paul's teaching on 'life by the Spirit' (Gal 5:16-25) contains his description of the fruit of the Spirit which reflects much of Jesus' character and how that is reproduced in us as we seek to 'live by the Spirit . . . keep in step with the Spirit'.

HIS WORDS: What Jesus said indeed proved to be words of life (John 6:68). He spoke plainly so all understood, always enabling the practical application (eg Matthew chapters 5, 6 and 7). They noted, along with the crowd, that when he spoke he had an influence, a power to engender obedience, an authority unlike any other teacher (Matt 7:28,29).

He used everyday events as real-life case studies (Mark 9:14-29;10:23-31). When they weren't at hand, he used parables, imaginary stories as case studies to earth their learning (Mark 4:1-34) – he blended cognitive and behavioural learning.

He **never compromised the truth** even when he knew it would offend and he would lose apparent supporters (John 6:60).

The disciples were admonished when they made mistakes (Matt 17:14-21), corrected when they thought wrongly (Matt 18:21,22; 19:13-15; Mark 16:14), affirmed for their increase in knowledge and discernment (Matt 16:17-19), and encouraged when they were successful (Luke 10:1-24).

Jesus also stressed to his disciples the indispensability of the empowerment of the Holy Spirit for every aspect of their being, words and deeds (John 14:15-17,25,26; 15:26; 16:5-15; Acts 1:4,5,8).

The disciples would heartily agree with the temple guards who were part of the conspiracy to destroy him, 'No-one ever spoke the way this man does' (John 7:46).

What a model to follow in mentoring!

HIS DEEDS: The disciples would echo the crowd's response to his **miracles**, 'We have never seen anything like this' (Mark 2:12).

The disciples soon became convinced that all Jesus' ministry was motivated by divine love. So he instructed them that love must be the badge of their discipleship, 'the very spring of all their actions', they must love as he loved (John 13:34; 15:12,13,17; 2 Cor 5:14).

They must have been almost overcome that Jesus entrusted his ministry to them with remarkable results. He practised mutual ministry, not to make his task lighter but to help them develop, in order to continue his ministry after his ascension (Matt 28:16-20; Mark 6:7-13). (Was Jesus inviting his disciples to actually perform the miracle of feeding the 5,000 when he said, 'You give them something to eat?' If so, they missed this mind-blowing opportunity when they looked to their own limited resources rather than trusting in God's – Mark 6:37,38). He chided them when they failed but stood by them, helping them to learn by reflecting on the event – Mark 9:14-29).

Christ's outcome was clear for mentoring those who were initially most unlikely future leaders. It was essentially to produce people who would witness to him as the clear priority for all they said and did (Acts 1:8).

And what remarkable witnesses and leaders the disciples became – prayerful, faithful, Christ-like, obedient, courageous, authoritative, full of compassion, effective in calling people to faith and nurturing and equipping them for ministry. They were instrumental in changing the course of history!

'All biblical mentoring then is under-mentoring. Jesus Christ is the real and decisive agent in Christian mentoring. We cannot bring about change in our mentorees, yet we can influence them to be changed by Jesus Christ. Therefore we must not regard him as the mentor of the past only, but as mentor in the present as well. Jesus' mentoring prototype is not merely a static blueprint of days past, it is operational as a formative power through the Holy Spirit today. In our day and age the Master's promise, 'Come follow me, and I will make you fish for people' (cf Matt 4:19) has lost neither its validity nor its authority.

'The Lord Jesus as our coaching model seeks more than our mere interest in him as an historical forerunner, he in fact claims our wholehearted trust in him as present enabler.'[3]

OTHER BIBLICAL MODELS

There are numerous examples of mentoring in the Scriptures – here are some of the better known ones. They give good guidelines for mentoring.

JETHRO AND MOSES

Jethro rescued his son-in-law from inevitable burnout by teaching him to delegate (Exod 18).

MOSES AND JOSHUA

Moses groomed Joshua for his mammoth task of leading Israel into the Promised Land (Deut 31:1-8; 34:9).

MOSES AND CALEB

Moses no doubt had a significant influence on Caleb, resulting in his becoming an outstanding leader, through to his senior years (Num 13; 14:6-9; 34:16-19; Josh 14:6-15).

SAMUEL AND SAUL

Samuel recognised great leadership potential in Saul and sought to mould and guide him, continuing to do so even after his spiritual demise (1 Sam 9:15).

SAMUEL AND DAVID

Samuel was clearly guided to David as a most unlikely leader initially, because of his age and stature. He then protected him from harm because of Saul's jealousy and mental instability (1Sam 16; 19:18-24).

JONATHAN AND DAVID

This was an equal relationship, with both receiving and giving. An excellent example of co-mentoring or peer mentoring in the depth of their commitment to each other and their families (1 Sam 18:1-4; 19:1-7; 20:1-42).

ELIJAH AND ELISHA

Elijah, who saw in Elisha someone who could continue his ministry, discipled him and eventually 'passed his baton' on to him. He was also open to be blessed by Elisha (1 Kings 19:16-21; 2 Kings 2:1-16; 3:11).

BARNABAS

Barnabas had a strong gift in encouragement. Indeed his name literally means 'son of encouragement' (Acts 4:36). He was a godly, joyous person. Acts 11:23,24 tells us he was Spirit-filled, a man of faith and an effective evangelist.

The Christian church owes so much to him for his mentoring of Paul. He recognised the potential in Paul when other believers distanced themselves from him after his conversion (Acts 9:27). He stood by Paul when he most needed a faithful friend (Acts 13:50) and celebrated with him when the church endorsed his ministry (Acts 13:2).

Barnabas stood by John Mark when he faltered, confronting Paul when he felt he was out of God's will in his handling of John Mark. He worked with him, enabling John Mark to eventually become a great support to Paul, and the one who many believe was the primary author of the gospel of Mark (Acts 15:36-39; 2 Tim 4:11).

I make a strong emphasis upon reflection as a most significant way to learn from our experiences. Was it Barnabas' reflections that made him depart from Paul? Reflection can be hazardous!

When Paul matured in ministry, Barnabas, like John the Baptist, was able to step aside and let him take centre stage (Acts 11:26 – cf Acts 13:50).

PAUL

Paul saw great promise in Timothy, so he mentored him, giving this emerging leader wise guidance and opportunities for hands-on experience as they travelled together. This resulted in the young church at Ephesus being enriched by having Timothy as their pastor. Luke says the churches in Lystra and Iconium spoke well of him (Acts 16:2). Paul's two letters to Timothy show some idea of how he discipled, instructed, encouraged and coached him (Phil 2:19-23).

PRISCILLA AND AQUILA WITH APOLLOS

Along with husband Aquila, Priscilla was one of the most distinguished of Paul's fellow-workers.

Of the five times her name is mentioned, three times it comes before that of her husband. It was believed that she was the more gifted and outstanding in leadership. Priscilla and Aquila both had profound knowledge of the Scriptures. They counselled and helped Apollos in his preaching methods and content, because of his weakness in these areas. 'They expounded to him the way of God more carefully' (Acts 18:26). The duration of the time of their friendship we do not know, but Apollos became a mighty spokesperson for the gospel and was called an apostle. The Corinthians put him before Peter and Paul. No doubt much of his success must be attributed to the wise and patient counsel of Priscilla and Aquila (Acts 18:2; 18:26; Rom 16:3; 1 Cor 16:19; 2 Tim 4:19).

EUNICE AND LOIS

As mother and grandmother, they must have mentored Timothy from a young age till he became a convert and mentoree of Paul. Eunice, having a Gentile husband, would have found in her mother, Lois, a source of encouragement, especially in Jewish matters, for both of these women were of the Jewish faith (Acts 16:1-3; 2 Tim 1-5; 3:14,15; 4:5).

---

[1] Eugene Petersen's, *The Message*, Navpress, Colarado, 1993
[2] This biblical background is based on a lecture given by Dr G S Dicker at a covenant-making workshop.
[3] *Mentoring for Mission*, Gunter Krallmann, Jensco Hong Kong & Globe Europe Missions, 1992

STUDY GUIDE

PERSONAL REFLECTION

1. What inspires you most about Jesus?
   - Why not pause now to worship him *(try to express how you feel about him, not just what you think of him)*.
2. What are a few things to guide you in your mentoring from the model Jesus provides for us?
   - Which of these are, to some degree, already characteristic of you?
   - Pause again to pray, thanking God for the way he has been making you more like Jesus.
3. Choose one of the Old Testament examples of mentoring. What can we learn from the way that was done?
4. Read both of Paul's letters to Timothy. List the major areas in which Paul helped this young leader.
5. What changes do you need to make for you to be a better model to those you seek to help?
   - How and when will you begin to work on these?

GROUP WORK

1. Allow group members to tell briefly what inspires them about Jesus. *(This could be followed by prayers of adoration and thanksgiving.)*
2. Collate on a chart or whiteboard the group's findings to 2 and 4 and discuss their relevance for mentoring today.
3. Use your work on the Old Testament examples to add to the above.

CHAPTER 3

UNDERSTANDING MENTORING

THE NEED FOR MENTORING

Of the 400 leaders in the Bible, only 100 finished well. So few finish well today. Rowland Croucher, of John Mark Ministries, Melbourne, claims his research reveals there are 10,000 ex-pastors in Australia! Although no doubt many are now in other forms of ministry, a significant number are not. The stresses of life and ministry, and the distractions of this world, have taken their toll. Many have been sidetracked, faded spiritually, or simply retreated.

Leaders, and indeed all faithful followers of Christ, will always continue to experience spiritual opposition as well as the everyday pressures of life.

The attitudes, behaviour and values of our post-modern world create unique tensions for those who seek to take the teachings of Jesus Christ seriously and propagate them. This contemporary thinking proclaims:

- There are no absolutes
- There is no abiding universal truth
- Traditional boundaries are gone
- Everyone is their own personal arbiter of what is right and wrong. All is purely subjective
- Family and religious values are either pushed to the fringe or rejected outright – there is little or no recognition of the values engendered in a reasonably secure family
- Authority and accountability are largely rejected

- Extreme forms of fundamentalism present an irrational way of responding
- There is despair because nothing really works any more. Technology and science have failed to perform in solving the world's problems.

Leaders have further expressed their need for mentoring because of the following:

- Pressures of public life
- Compulsive, competitive behaviour
- Ego-driven 'big-shots'!
- Irresistible forces of power (pride), wealth (greed), sex (lust)
- Western culture's individualism/independence
- Cynical spirit of today's media and society
- Neglect of friends, spouse and family
- Few meaningful relationships
- Inexperience
- Little or no intimacy with Christ
- Lack of discipline and accountability
- Difficulty in breaking one's isolation and becoming transparent and vulnerable even within a caring group
- Personality problems – poor relational skills, insecurity, timidity, etc
- Positive learning attitude missing
- Loss of perspective – the big picture
- For males, loss of male identity and traditional roles as a result of the strengthening women's movement.

For further reading

It would be useful to read a reliable book on post-modernity, if you have not already done so, to be better able to understand and communicate with others. Avoid books which take an irrational stance.

Suggested reading: *Post Modernity*, David Lyon, Open University Press, 1995; *Faith and Modernity*, edited by Philip Sampson, Vinay Samuel and Chris Sugden, Regnum Books International, 1994.

STUDY GUIDE

PERSONAL REFLECTION

1. Tick any of the above which indicate pressures you personally experience, and list additional reasons why you feel the need for a mentor?
   - In what ways do these affect you?
2. How does it (could it) help you in coping with the above by having someone with whom you can (could) share openly and pray?
3. What role does your relationship to God play in meeting these needs?

GROUP WORK

1. Share any of your individual work about which you feel comfortable.
2. Identify any items in the above list which apply to all or most Christian believers, not just to leaders.
3. How would you seek to help your co-mentor or a mentoree in meeting one or more of these needs?

—✳✳✳—

THE HEART OF CHRISTIAN MENTORING
HELPING THE DEVELOPMENT OF A GROWING RELATIONSHIP WITH GOD

God is not apart from his world, but ever-present, Emmanuel – God with us – in every circumstance of life. John's gospel uniquely introduces us to God as the God who communicates, who expresses himself to his people. God is a relational, loving, communicating God. Jesus is the 'Word' made flesh to communicate God's will and purposes through who he is and what he did as well as what he said. To fulfil our purpose on earth we must take unhurried time to listen, to understand and respond appropriately in faith. So life and ministry are meant to be an unending Emmaus Road experience – walking with Jesus, letting him have our undivided attention so that our hearts may 'burn within us', being ignited by his words and his presence.

46

> **Mentoring is concerned essentially with assisting a person to recognise and respond to the prompting of God's Spirit so that the mind and power of Christ may govern all a person is and does in order to arrive at the goal to which God is leading. It is about enabling another to 'live and keep in step with the Spirit' (Gal 5:25).**

Christian mentoring is about enabling a person to develop a growing, working relationship with God through all he has done for us in Christ. Enabling a mentoree to slow down and allow God to get their attention should be the central focus. The mentoree must be helped, not so much to try to better understand their relationship with God, but to engage in it, to enter into dialogue with God, to listen to what God has to say, especially through the Scriptures, but also through the Christian community (friends, leaders, mentors, etc) and through prayer and the context in which we live and work.

Some mentoring, spiritual direction, coaching, discipling, concentrates on advice giving, upon the giving of specific, often inflexible, instructions on how to act and live. The impression given is that the answers to life's dilemmas and challenges lie within the adviser.

Others take a totally non-directive approach, believing that all we need to do as helpers is to ask the right questions to enable a person to arrive at the right conclusions – 'the answers and the power are within you'. None of these approaches are entirely inappropriate. There will be times when we will use both.

However, authentic Christian mentoring sees the relationship between two people as only a means to an end. The end is God – his grace, his glory, his purposes. The assumption is that God and the person can work it out together! Our role is always secondary to that.

When Paul says, 'we proclaim him, admonishing and teaching everyone with all wisdom, so that we may present everyone **mature in Christ**' (Col 1:28), he clearly understands his role as that of enabling ongoing transformation in those he nurtured through God's grace. Mentoring seeks to facilitate this coming into being. Mentors challenge and inspire others to keep going deeper, to allow themselves to be loved and to love, to take greater 'risks' of faith and to become more actively engaged with God in his reckless love for all humankind.

With those who were taking **first steps** in their Christian walk, Paul describes this task in terms of 'mother' ('nurse') and 'father' (1 Thess 2:7-12). Mentors of beginners in the Christian life need to be especially sensitive and understanding, not expecting too much, understanding any limitations, protective yet able to challenge and facilitate growth, ready to affirm every good effort and always encouraging (see Chapter 6, 'Mentoring New Christians', p 147).

Ongoing discipling seeks to facilitate continuing growth in knowledge of Christ as Lord, and deepening commitment and obedience to him. Increased understanding of the Bible and its application to life and ministry will also be encouraged. Discovery, development and use of spiritual gifts and equipping for appropriate ministries in both the church and the world is essential for disciples if they are to participate in Christ's mission. Discipling of others will also endeavour to enable the steady emergence of an authentic Christian style of living. Familiarity with other Christian resources will further help the disciple fulfil God's purposes.

STUDY GUIDE

PERSONAL REFLECTION – on your life experiences, with God

LIST 10 KEY EVENTS in your life from birth to now	LIST THE MAIN DETAILS of the event	FIND ONE WORD FOR EACH EVENT that expresses significance

1. In what ways has God's past action in your life (recalled above) moulded your current attitudes/values/behaviour?
2. What practical steps do you (can you) take to allow God to get your attention on a regular basis?
3. What questions would you ask a person whom you are mentoring to encourage them to reflect on their growing relationship to God?

GROUP WORK

1. Share your responses to the above.
2. Take aspects of what was shared about developing a growing relationship with God. Work out how you would explain this to a new follower of Christ in simple terms, without it being burdensome or legalistic.

—✳✳✳—

MENTORING AS A DYNAMIC SYSTEM

There are three ways in which a person can be involved in a mentoring network. Ideally a person should endeavour to be engaged in each of these aspects at one and the same time to balance the receiving in personal mentoring relationships with a giving of support and encouragement to others.

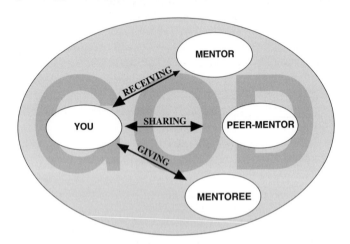

A RECEIVING RELATIONSHIP

In this dimension of mentoring we enter into a relationship with a more mature, more experienced person, who has been faithful in the long haul. They become our mentor and we, as mentorees, benefit from their wise advice, modelling and encouragement.

'Mentors speak three messages: It can be done!

You're not alone!

I believe in you'.[1]

Mentors may also sponsor their mentorees by giving them openings to widen their experience, making contacts with other significant leaders and involving them in new areas of ministry.

A SHARING RELATIONSHIP

This involves **co-mentoring** with a peer, a person of similar age and interest and commitment to Christ.

It is an *equal* relationship between two people who value and respect each other and believe each can enrich the other.

The relationship is usually less formal than the previous example or the following one. Often it simply involves making a present friendship more intentional by knowing the right questions to ask, sharing openly and honestly and keeping one another accountable. This ought to be an enjoyable, relaxed relationship, with a fun dimension.

Unfortunately this readily available and most effective form of mentoring is overlooked by many or not developed to its full potential.

This sharing relationship can sometimes be fulfilled in a small group, the smaller the better – three or four is an ideal number.

A Giving Relationship

Here we develop a relationship with a less experienced person exercising a similar role to the mentor in the receiving relationship. This person becomes our **mentoree**.

Sometimes this person will seek us out, but often we need to take the initiative with those who may benefit from our help. As we actively listen to people we may hear their silent or spoken cries for help and offer to stand with them.

Being in this three-dimensional network helps us maintain the balance of authentic Christian discipleship through receiving and giving. It can also lessen the possibility that dependency could develop.

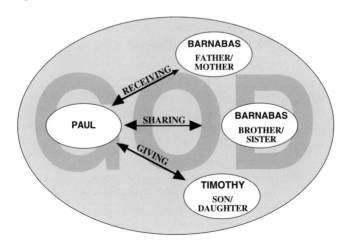

Paul and **Barnabas** illustrate these three ways of mentoring. When considering biblical models in the previous chapter, we recalled how initially Barnabas was a **mentor** to the newly converted Paul, helping others recognise the genuine transformation that had taken place in this former persecutor of the new church. Being the person he was, Barnabas no doubt made a big impact on Paul through his warm fellowship, wise counsel, encouragement, protection and sponsoring of Paul before the church leaders. Barnabas was like a **spiritual parent** to Paul in the early stages of his Christian experience.

Later, they ministered together, sharing the adversities as well as the joys of serving in previously unreached places. Travelling together, they would share their experiences, pray together, discuss many issues so new to them both and talk often of their Lord. There was both giving and receiving in a peer mentoring relationship. They were like **spiritual siblings** – brothers in Christ.

Paul recognised emerging leaders and was soon mentoring the likes of Timothy, Titus and many others. These mentorees benefited from Paul's wisdom, his clear grasp of the gospel, his varied experiences in ministry to his broad networks. They became like his **spiritual offspring** – sons and daughters in the faith.

Paul's writings to these two young leaders show how he made them **reflect** seriously about their ministry, lifestyle and relationship to Christ.

The two diagrams used here also seek to emphasise again that **God is the mentor**. All effective Christian mentoring takes place under the guidance and empowerment of God, who always takes the initiative – going before to prepare the way, and always with us.

STUDY GUIDE

PERSONAL REFLECTION

1. What experiences have you had, however briefly, past or present, which fit into any of these dimensions of mentoring?
   • How helpful were/are they?
2. Has anyone spoken to you the 'three messages' listed by Crabb?

- How did it make you feel?
- How did it help?
- Have you been able to speak these to another person? How did they respond?

3. What are some things that Paul and Barnabas might have talked about as mutual mentors (hard questions asked of each other/words to encourage)?

4. What have your learnt from this reflection to help you in mentoring?

GROUP WORK

1. Share together any of the above individual work.

2. You may want to role-play Paul and Barnabas mutually mentoring each other in ways suggested in the fourth-last paragraph of the above text. Or better still, choose a situation recorded in Acts chapters 13 and 14, where they are together.

—✳✳✳—

PEER MENTORING

'Two are better than one, because they have a good reward for their toil. For if they fall, one will lift up the other; but woe to one who is alone and falls and does not have another to help . . . and though one might prevail against another, two will withstand one. A threefold cord is not quickly broken.' (Eccl 4:9,10,12)

Peer mentoring involves co-mentoring with a person of similar age, interests and commitment to Christ. The relationship is the most accessible of the three ways a person can be involved in mentoring. Unlike the other two, which focus mainly on receiving or giving, this is a **shared relationship**, involving both giving and receiving.

> **It is an equal relationship between two people who value and respect each other and believe each can enrich the other.**

The relationship is usually less formal, more convenient and flexible than the other two forms of mentoring. Often it simply involves making more of a present friendship while retaining the enjoyable, easygoing, fun dimension of such a close relationship.

Peer mentoring helps us face the reality about both our good and our bad aspects. We are rescued from self-deception concerning the public and private areas of our lives. A real friend can work with us in dealing with the major areas where we can stray and enable us to overcome poor self-esteem, lack of confidence and the many other things that prevent us from being the person God wants us to be in Christ.

The 'one another' and 'together' passages of the New Testament can usually be lived out at a greater level of intimacy in peer mentoring relationships. Carrying each other's burden (Gal 6:1,2), building each other up in Christ (1 Thess 5:11), encouraging each other to love and serve (Heb 10:24,25), protecting each other from sin (Heb 3:12-14), listening to each other's confession of sin (Jas 5:16) and showing genuine compassion to each other (John 13:34,35; 1 John 3:11) are more easily achievable and have a greater depth with one other person than with a group or crowd.

The effectiveness of these relationships is because of the unrestricted openness, trust, commitment, sense of responsibility for each other and mutual accountability which is already present in good friendships and which can be developed further when there is an agreement to be more purposeful.

> **Unfortunately this so readily available, and most effective, form of mentoring is overlooked by many or not developed to its full potential.**

A BIBLICAL MODEL

David and Jonathan provide the best example of peer-mentoring in the Scriptures. Both had much in common. They were brave, courageous, upright, God-fearing men. Their friendship was characterised by oneness of spirit, transparency and a deep commitment to protect each other and their families. Implicit trust, encouragement and love were also clearly evident in the way they related (See 1 Sam, chapters 16–23, especially 18:1,3; 20:3,4, 14-17, 42; 23:16,17).

BEGIN WITH A FRIEND

Most friendships involve varying degrees of informal mentoring – we just need to become a little more intentional for the relationship to become more effective in producing encouragement, support, confidence and transformation.

Take the initiative with a close friend by making yourself vulnerable by openly and honestly sharing a dream or passion, a deep experience, an inner struggle or an area of your life you have never felt free to talk about previously.

Friendships can sometimes be less than helpful because in listening to a person re-tell the same problem each time you meet, you may find yourself reinforcing the issue rather than enabling them to face up to it. Simply asking your friend, 'What do you think you could be doing about this?' or, 'What could God be wanting you to do about this with his help (and mine)?' could help them identify and begin to deal with their situation. By becoming more intentional, with sensitivity you could become God's agent of hope and transformation. Your friend, by playing a similar role for you, could help make the relationship one of co-mentoring.

However, be careful not to put the relationship under undue pressure. If it has been an effective mentoring relationship to date, then don't sacrifice the friendship by making a formal structure.

Peer mentoring should maintain a high degree of informality. As with most good friendships, it will involve snacks and meals together and relaxed, recreational activities, such as walking together, playing golf, etc.

SET ASIDE REGULAR TIMES TO BE TOGETHER

Re-arrange your schedule and activities so that you have adequate time to build a relationship that moves deeper than the relatively superficial level of most friendships.

A mutual commitment to meet regularly helps develop the relationship by enabling up-to-date reporting back to each other and ongoing support.

MAXIMISE YOUR TIMES TOGETHER

Maintain a balance in your relationship. Don't be too hard or too easy with each other. Seek to avoid becoming too intense so that a good friendship is spoilt, or by being too easy with each other so that the relationship is too superficial for significant changes to occur. Also keep in mind that this is an **equal** relationship.

Seek to be transparent with each other. Don't force this, just let the Spirit lead you gently! Share your disappointments and frustration and celebrate together your joys and successes.

In seeking to deepen your degree of vulnerability and intimacy with each other, understanding **the five levels of communication** on which people relate can be helpful. These move from the least to the most intimate.

Level 1 – Stereotyped or hackneyed expressions:

Each culture has its standard greeting between strangers which does not expect an in-depth reply. This is the level of conversation in an elevator or a social gathering with strangers. Permissible topics are the news, weather, sports, etc. It is 'talking without speaking' and 'hearing without listening'. There are no emotions or opinions expressed.

Level 2 – Communication of facts:

Little if anything of our real selves is exposed. We report what others have said or done without expressing any feelings, giving anything of ourselves or expecting a reply.

Level 3 – Disclosing ideas and judgments:

We risk telling another person some dreams, ideas, judgments and decisions which are important to us, but quickly back off if interest is not shown. We feel confident to continue to the next level if there is acceptance.

Level 4 – Revealing feelings:

The feelings or emotions which lie under our convictions are revealed. We share thoughts and feelings about our struggles, fears and anxieties.

Level 5 – Oneness:

This most intimate level of sharing is the depth of relationship referred to in the New Testament as 'the fellowship of the Holy Spirit' (*koinonia*). It is based on total openness and honesty about each other's thoughts and feelings and is accompanied by tremendous joy and satisfaction.

As Christians, we believe this unique experience of communion with each other is produced by being fully open to the presence of the Holy Spirit in our friendship.

FOCUS ON MAJOR AREAS WHERE WE CAN STRAY
- Friendships
- Spouse and family
- Self-centredness
- Management of time
- Pride – self-image
- Lust
- Greed – attitude towards money
- Honesty
- Power
- Acknowledgment of authority
- Servanthood
- Availability for service

ASK GOOD QUESTIONS
Help each other to think by asking good questions, including the tough ones. See the section which gives a range of questions in Chapter 5, p 124. Don't let each other get away with anything – be gentle but direct and incisive (Heb 10:24, 'Spur one another on . . .' But remember Christ's teaching about 'specks' and 'logs' (Matt 7:1-5)!

BE MUTUALLY ACCOUNTABLE
In being accountable to each other constantly monitor legalism and moralism to avoid being driven by 'law' rather than the grace of the gospel. (See 'Walking the Road Together', p 34, for more on accountability.)

SHOW MUTUAL RESPECT
Accept each other unconditionally, so neither will fear rejection no matter what happens. Allow each other space to develop in the way God intends.

TAKE SCRIPTURE SERIOUSLY
Don't just use Scripture as a box of promises or bandaids. Explore its relevance for the matters you deal with and nudge each other to put it into practice with the help of God's Spirit.

PRAY TOGETHER

Pray about the specific issues shared. Pray that out of this developing relationship your love and trust for each other, and God, will become credible and grow. Pray each time you are together and in between. Use your phone for prayer with each other.

LAUGH TOGETHER, CRY TOGETHER, HAVE FUN TOGETHER!

As we become more transparent with each other, feelings of joy and sorrow will naturally surface. When masks disappear there grows an ability to laugh at ourselves and each other and also to shed tears without embarrassment.

Build in plenty of serendipity for each other, those happy, unexpected surprises. Have plenty of fun together!

ARRANGE SOME SPECIAL TIMES TOGETHER

From time to time, arrange to spend an extended time together for a retreat in an entirely different setting. This could vary from a few hours to one or more days. (There are many resources available to help make the most of such times.) While it may be agreed to fast on these occasions, learn to 'party' also.

PEER MENTORING IN SMALL GROUPS

This is an extension of peer co-mentoring which provides a broader base for the experience. See the section in Chapter 6, p 150 'Mentoring and Small Groups' for suggestions on how to strengthen certain types of small groups, such as pairing members in co-mentoring relationships, and for other ideas.

STUDY GUIDE

PERSONAL REFLECTION

1. In what ways has a close friend encouraged or strengthened you?
   • What 'feeling' words would you use to describe this relationship?
2. Two of the greatest barriers to entering into an open, deep relationship with a peer are fear and pride. How true do you think this is? How true is it of you?

3. What would you hope to receive from a peer-mentoring relationship?

4. What could you give to a peer-mentoring relationship?
   • What would this involve for you?

5. What did you find most helpful in 'Maximise Your Times Together'? How was it helpful?

GROUP WORK

1. Begin by sharing your stories (from above).

2. Two barriers to openness are given:
   • Share your responses
   • What other barriers are there?

3. Discuss 'Maximise Your Times Together'.

4. Regarding where we can stray, which of the major areas given would you find the hardest to be transparent about with another, or with a small group?

—✳✳✳—

MAJOR AREAS OF MENTORING

Here are some common areas in which people seek mentoring:
• Development of spiritual life
   Setting aside adequate time in a busy schedule
   How to pray more effectively
   How to understand the Bible and take it more seriously
   Practising other spiritual disciplines
   Developing your own unique form of spirituality
   Living and walking in the Spirit
• Giving quality time to those closest to you – friends, spouse, family
• Management of time and creative use of leisure
• Setting priorities and goals
• Choosing between the good and the best in your life and Christian service
• Personal and professional development
• Attitude towards, and use of, money
• Handling power with grace and humility

- Sexual relationships
- Remaining open and honest
- Coping with stress
- Keeping positive and hopeful
- Self-control
- Resolving conflicts
- Relating well to people.

STUDY GUIDE

PERSONAL REFLECTION
1. What would you add to this list?
2. In which of the above areas would you appreciate help?
   - In what ways?
   - Who do you think could help you?
   - When will you approach them?

GROUP WORK
Share as much of the above as makes you feel comfortable.

—✳✳✳—

DISPELLING SOME MYTHS
'I'm too young'
   Age is not a factor. You may have resources (see Chapter 4, 'Our Personal Mentoring Resources', p 90) which match the needs of another. Also, remember Paul's counsel to young Timothy, 'Let no one despise your youth, but set the believers an example in speech and conduct, in love, in faith, in purity' (1 Tim 4:12).

'I'm too inexperienced'
   If you have a healthy, growing relationship to God you can be used to support and encourage others in a peer relationship or in discipling/mentoring a new or immature Christian. You don't have to be 'a professional' or a spiritual giant. When you are in a situation which is beyond you, you can be a channel to other more resourced, more experienced, more mature people.

60

'I lack confidence'

You don't have to make it on your own. As is explained elsewhere, God is the mentor; our role is to be available for him to work through us. As the psalmist says: 'My help comes from the Lord who made heaven and earth' (Wow!) Ps 121:1,2.

'I could give the impression I'm superior to the one I'm trying to help'

I hear this frequently from women. Each one has been a humble, mature, godly, prayerful person who has so much to offer. The New Testament affirms the very significant role of women in mentoring. Priscilla is always mentioned in the New Testament with her husband Aquila as ministering together, assisting Paul and mentoring Apollos at Ephesus, enabling him to become one of the most powerful spokespersons for the Christian gospel. Eunice and Lois, Timothy's mother and grandmother, mentored him from an early age until he became a mentoree of Paul. Each time women are shown in a mentoring role, with men or women, there is no hint of superiority.

'I can't locate the right people'

God hasn't lost the address of those who need to be helped – all their needs are known to him and he is well able to meet them through people who allow themselves to be guided to where he is already at work.

Read the encouraging words of Jesus in Matthew 6:25-34 (note the condition in verse 33).

'The people I think of who could mentor me are too busy'

Don't make up other people's minds for them. Don't pre-judge another's availability. If it's the right person, they will be accessible. Test the waters! 'Ask', 'Seek', 'Knock'! And don't quit if the first person you contact is genuinely too busy.

'I'm too busy'

Mentoring is usually undertaken by busy people! Begin by mentoring one person. Select carefully this person and follow the guidelines given to maximise your times together. Meet at times outside your normally busy periods – such as over breakfast, lunch, supper – indeed I know of one leader who has his mentoring sessions at 5.00 am! Limit the time for each meeting to an hour and meet monthly. Try meeting for six to eight times, then evaluate – extend the period if it has been worthwhile and you can give more time.

People who are too busy to meet with a peer for mutual support are too busy!

'I'm housebound and can't get out to meet others'

Many effective mentors are housebound by a young family or some disability.

'A mentoree could become too dependent on me'

Healthy mentoring encourages mentorees to take responsibility for their own lives. It may build up a mentor's ego to find the person being dependent, but it is a very unhelpful relationship for both.

Good mentoring involves reflection to help the recipient own their situation and to explore options to deal with it.

'I feel some concern about committing myself to another for an extended period'

Some mentoring relationships, especially with a more mature person and with a less mature person, may exist for only a relatively short period. It is important to set an initial time frame that can be extended or shortened as you keep evaluating the effectiveness of the relationship.

'One needs to have a lot in common with a mentor/mentoree'

While there needs to be some degree of compatibility to enable bonding, diversity can bring an objectivity, freshness and breadth of perspective.

---

[1] *The Silence of Adam*, Lawrence Crabb, Zondervan, 1995

STUDY GUIDE

PERSONAL REFLECTION
1. Have any of the above 'myths' been a problem for you personally?
   • If so, why?
   • How did you handle it?

GROUP WORK
1. Discuss the above.
2. List any other myths you can think of, and discuss.

CHAPTER 4

WHAT IT TAKES TO BE A MENTOR

BASIC QUALITIES OF A MENTOR

There are certain basic qualities that are found in successful mentors. From my own observation and conversations with many mentors and mentorees, I came up with over sixty characteristics! The following seeks to gather most of these into a more manageable list. This list is still somewhat formidable and could turn some away from attempting this rewarding work. However, inadequacy is a feeling common to many of the people God uses in exceptional ways (see Chapter 2, 'Having a Sane Estimate of Yourself and Others', p 30).

No mentor possesses any of these qualities to the degree that there is no more room for growth. A basic characteristic of good mentors assumed here is that they are persons who are continually becoming. Like Paul they can say, 'I haven't arrived, but I have a clear goal and am pressing towards it' (Phil 3:12-14).

CHRIST-CENTRED

This is the foundational quality for Christian mentoring. What is essential for a disciplemaker is a life touched and being continually renewed by Jesus Christ. Then ordinary abilities become extraordinary. The most searching question I have ever been asked is, 'Do you really love Jesus Christ?' My greatest challenge is to keep my relationship with Christ fresh and growing. This is our secret centre, 'the very spring of our actions' (Prov 4:23).

Jesus said, 'Apart from me you can do nothing' (John 15:5). The corollary of this statement is that with Christ the impossible is within our grasp – we can be different and make a difference. More than anything else, our mentorees need living, demonstrable evidence of that.

One of my mentorees said that what he looks for most in a mentor is a person who will never let him lose his focus on deepening his relationship to Jesus Christ. Our goal is not to build their attachment to ourselves but to Christ.

Passionate

Passion is what drives us. It is the strong enthusiasm we have for something. Some people are passionate about their families, sport, garden, music or art. To be really effective in mentoring, we need a passion for it, not to do it just because it's 'the flavour of the month' or we felt it was 'the right thing to do'.

Some say the need is the call. In a sense that is right, but to undertake something purely to meet a need can mean it is done grudgingly, out of a sense of duty. There are tasks that I find hard to get passionate about – such as tidying the office, filing, paying bills or weeding the garden!

Passion for any form of ministry can grow the more we understand what it entails and recognise its potential – as we catch the vision. I have found my enthusiasm and zeal for mentoring keeps growing the more I'm involved with emerging leaders, seeing the encouragement they receive and the transformation which takes place in their lives and ministries. I'm passionate about mentoring because, more than ever, I understand it, know how to go about it and regularly see evidence of how effective it can be.

Although we need a passion to mentor, initially it may be little more than a leaning in that direction as we begin to understand and see the need for mentoring. The enthusiasm, the zeal, may grow as you get involved and see the remarkable difference even an hour or two a month with a mentoree can make.

However, not everyone is meant to mentor, so if after reading this book you don't feel you have a leaning towards it, think again about becoming involved. Or, if after you do get started, there is no eagerness and it becomes a burden to you, then you should withdraw after passing your mentoree on to another.

RELATIONAL

Mentors need to be able to establish and maintain relationships. They should know how to **develop rapport**, to get alongside, to empathise, to help people feel at ease. Love is shown by the way they **actively listen**. Mentorees are accepted for who they are, not for what they do or don't do. They can inspire and motivate by their attitude and behaviour.

Mentors are interested and concerned about their mentoree's family and friends, and will frequently ask questions about them during regular meetings. Phone calls to the home of the mentoree present an opportunity to talk informally to the spouse and children. This bond can be deepened where a meal together can be arranged.

Relational people give the impression they **enjoy being with others** and they are **always out to encourage**. Their personal security is such that they can allow the other person their freedom and are not threatened when the other does things better. This quality is not limited to the extroverts. Often the introverted, shy person finds it easier to exercise these traits.

Opportunities for emotional release are provided. Times to laugh and to cry are seen as a normal part of the process.

AFFIRMING

Mentors believe in their mentorees and tell them so. They have an ability to discern potential and enable its development by their ongoing commitment, support, affirmation of every genuine effort and by turning failures into learning experiences. They love celebrating their mentorees' successes!

OPEN AND TRANSPARENT

Mentors are **believable** – there is integrity in who they are, what they say and what they do. They never seek to come across as superior, paragons of virtue or 'know-it-alls'. They are honest about their failures and weaknesses, as well as their successes. They are growing people who are open to learn from their mentorees – and to tell them when they do! Mentorees find it easy to identify with them.

Mentors know when to ask the **tough questions** to help their mentorees think frankly about themselves and the way they do things. They know when to be direct and to reprimand if responses indicate the process is not being taken seriously. Warnings are given about dangers ahead and wrongs confronted. But mentors 'speak the truth in love' so as never to discourage or cause loss of confidence – it is always done to foster growth.

TRUSTING AND TRUSTWORTHY

Mentors are **trusting and trustworthy**. They trust the word of their charge and trust them to carry out their responsibilities. Mentors keep confidences.

AVAILABLE

The frequency of face-to-face meetings will be by mutual agreement – every four to six weeks is common, but contact may be more frequent. It is important that the mentor can be relied upon, in normal circumstances, to meet these agreed commitments.

Assurance will be given that extra contacts can be made if a special need arises. When a mentoree is struggling with a particularly difficult issue, I often phone to check how they are going and to share a prayer.

The length of time the relationship is regularly maintained will vary – some continue for a six-month period, others for far longer. Often an irregular ongoing relationship is maintained for many years after the intensive period.

I mentor many who live in other states or other countries. Most of the mentoring is done by phone, e-mail or letter. When I travel to these areas, I set up face-to-face meetings in advance.

ABLE TO FACILITATE LEARNING

Mentors know how to help mentorees learn. They are not quick to give advice. Good questions are used to probe and enable reflection so that mentorees are made to think for themselves and learn from their life experiences. The agenda of the mentoree guides the time together. Dreaming, seeing possibilities, exploring options, working through issues and setting goals occupies much of the time together.

Good mentors ask at the appropriate moments, 'What do you think Jesus would do here?' 'How can the Scriptures guide us in this?' This helps the mentorees see the Scriptures as our primary, proven resource for our spirituality and ministry.

COMPETENT

A mentor needs to be capable in the areas in which the mentoree wants to grow. The areas of competency in which help is sought can be wide-ranging. A young mother finding difficulty in her new role forms a relationship with an older godly woman from whom she receives wise guidance and support. A minister with obvious preaching gifts benefits from meeting with a competent preacher to improve his/her skills. The mentoree will seek out a person who, in their eyes, has been successful, someone they admire, respect, see as a model and can imitate.

PRAYERFUL

Prayer is not an add-on for a good mentor – it is, in the words of the old hymn, the mentor's 'vital breath'.

'Praying is not simply some necessary compartment in the daily schedule of a Christian or a source of support in time of need, nor is it restricted to Sunday morning . . . Prayer leads one to see new paths and hear new melodies in the air. Prayer is the breath of one's life, which gives you freedom to go . . . and to find many signs which point out the way to a new land. Praying is living.'[1]

Prayer will occupy an important place in each mentoring session, for often there will be no easy answers to the issues discussed. A fresh touch from Christ may be needed to heal wounds and renew hope, or to raise a duet of praise for God's faithfulness. The mentors' own prayer lists will include their mentorees' needs. This may prompt a prayer together over the phone in between face-to-face meetings.

STUDY GUIDE
PERSONAL REFLECTION
1. Think of two or three people who have helped you significantly in your Christian life and/or your service. Which qualities were their strongest?
2. On the graph below, try to estimate how evident these qualities are in you.

Weak	1	2	3	4	5	6	7	8	9	10 *Strong*
Christ-centred										
Passionate										
Relational										
Affirming										
Open, transparent										
Help learning										
Available										
Prayerful										

3. Which of the above presents the greatest challenge to you? Before you commence mentoring, you may need to discuss this with another leader.
   - Who will you choose?
   - When will you do this?
4. What is your area of competency in life skills and/or ministry?

GROUP WORK
1. Share as much of your individual work as you are able with a partner.
2. How important do you think the relational aspect is in mentoring?
   - What suggestions are made about the ways in which rapport is developed?
   - What would you add to these?
3. What are the disadvantages of lack of openness by both mentor and mentoree?
   - What, if any, limits should there be to openness? (See below, 'Sharpening our Self-Awareness: The Hidden Quadrant', p 73.)
4. What are the main points made about availability?
   - What limits should be made to one's availability?
   - When, if ever, should these limits be broken?
5. What would you add to the list of basic qualities?

—✳✳✳—

SHARPENING OUR SELF-AWARENESS

As a mentor, you are, effectively, your own tool of trade. The quality and integrity of your mentoring will therefore be an extension of how well-tuned and honed that tool is. The best mentors are those who function from deep self-awareness and a strong commitment to self-growth. I cannot take someone where I haven't been myself, and I cannot minister to others out of my own emptiness. Mentoring subsequently grows out of, and is a direct reflection of, my own self-awareness.

This is not to say that mentors have arrived in their own journey towards self-discovery; we are, and will always be, fellow pilgrims on the way. However, mentors need to be able to claim the following:

> I know myself.
> I accept myself.
> I can forget myself.

Only then are mentors able to facilitate self-discovery and growth in others.

One model which is invaluable in helping us determine our own level of self-awareness is the **Johari Window**. The following exercises will allow you to construct this window, and then we will explore the implications of it for you as a mentor.

STUDY GUIDE

PERSONAL REFLECTION

Firstly, draw a straight horizontal line, numbered from 0 to 10, as follows:

0 _____ 10

Then place an X on the line to indicate how open you believe you are to feedback from others, with 0 representing not being open to feedback at all, and 10 representing being totally open and receptive, to the point of frequently soliciting feedback about yourself from others. If, for example, I think that I get quite defensive when others give me feedback (about my performance, personality or behaviour), tending to either disregard what they say or become annoyed, I would place an X at 2 or 3 on the line, as follows:

0____ x _____ 10

Next, draw a vertical line downwards of equal length to form a right angle with the horizontal line, as indicated below:

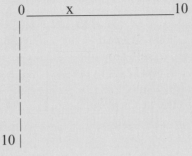

Place another X on this second line to indicate how easily and freely you share information about yourself with others generally. If, for example, I think I am an up-front person who volunteers information about myself so that people will know me beyond superficial layers, I'd place an X at around the 8 or 9 point on the line. Finally, draw two lines to complete the outside of the square, and draw in two other lines to join up the two X's, as follows. You should end up with one large square, with four areas of differing sizes within it.

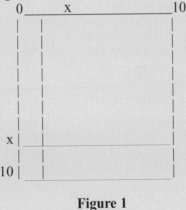

Figure 1

What you have just completed is your own configuration of the Johari Window, an instrument devised by two sociologists (named Joe and Harry!). It provides a lens through which we can look into the self. The four areas within the window have been individually named, as follows:

JOHARI WINDOW

	Known to me	Not known to me
Known by others	*OPEN*	*BLIND*
Not known by others	*HIDDEN*	*UNKNOWN*

Figure 2

1. **The open self:** what I am aware of in myself (mannerisms, thoughts, feelings, beliefs, experiences, etc), and which others are also aware of, either because it is obvious or because I have freely shared this information about myself with them.
2. **The blind self:** those aspects of myself to which I am oblivious but which are (sometimes painfully!) obvious to others. These represent my personal blind spots.
3. **The hidden or concealed self:** information about myself that I withhold or try to hide from others. Perhaps I came from the sort of family that encouraged a stiff-upper-lip approach to life; or maybe I've been vulnerable in the past and had my trust betrayed, thus causing me now to hold things in. Conversely, some people who have low self-esteem hide their true self behind a mask for fear of rejection.
4. **The unknown self:** once described as 'the God-only-knows-box'. This is the realm of my hidden potential, the unconscious, and my repressed memories.

The configuration of the four areas in Figure 1 refers to people who are dominated by quadrant 2, the **blind** area. The implications of this are that these people have many blind spots about how they relate to others, are viewed by others, and function in their role.

> *PERSONAL REFLECTION* (continued)
> What is the dominant quadrant in your Johari Window configuration?
> What might be some of the implications of this for you as a mentor?

A mentor whose Johari Window looks like Figure 1, for instance, appears to be so lacking in self-awareness that it is likely that he/she would not be optimising the effectiveness and value of the mentoring process.

> *PERSONAL REFLECTION* (continued)
> What blind spots could a mentor have which could reduce the benefits of the mentoring process? (eg the tendency to interrupt others, distracting mannerisms, gender bias, 'wandering' eyes, poor attending skills.)

Here are some ways in which the **blind quadrant** can be reduced:
• intentionally commit yourself to a growing self-awareness;
• monitor habits, idiosyncrasies, behavioural patterns and traits;
• examine yourself (and your mentoring relationships) periodically for possible subconscious motivations and hidden agenda;
• invite significant people in your life to give you specific feedback about personality and performance issues, then reflect on what they tell you;
• learn to trust and accept others' perceptions about you.

The **hidden quadrant** is what I know about myself but don't want you to know. It is reduced by being committed to appropriate self-disclosure. In the case of self-disclosure in mentoring, however, a proviso needs to be stipulated. Obviously, people with a small hidden quadrant would be comfortable sharing information about themselves and their own journey, a trait one would normally view as an asset in building meaningful relationships.

However, studies of the helping professions are indicating that inappropriate (excessive) self-disclosure by counsellors to their clients is a reliable predictor of whether or not that counsellor will violate professional boundaries and become romantically and/or sexually involved with a client.

As mentors, we need to constantly monitor how much of our own journey we share with mentorees. If we feel the need to share a lot of details about our own experience, we must address two vital questions:

1. Is the fact that I have hijacked the mentoring process with my own story an indication that I have personal work I need to complete before I am free to access another's story?

2. Am I talking so much about myself because I am (even unconsciously) seeking a form of two-way intimacy with the mentoree in order to meet some of my unmet personal needs?

The only valid reason mentors have in sharing their own story is to aid the mentoree in some way. If it is merely an indulgence, or some egocentric desire to switch the focus back to themselves, it is out of place in the mentoring process.

Here are some ways in which the **hidden quadrant** can be reduced:

• commit yourself to a growing honesty and vulnerability;
• learn to trust more;
• accept yourself as you are – in process;
• examine yourself (and your mentoring relationships) periodically for your motivations and intentional hidden agenda;
• reflect on the reasons you might wish or need to hide matters, as you become aware of this occurring.

The issues of self-awareness and self-disclosure are vital for the effective mentor. Self-awareness is vital because mentors don't want lack of self-knowledge to become a barrier to an optimal mentoring relationship. Self-disclosure is vital because that is precisely what mentors are inviting of their mentorees. Mentors therefore need to understand the dynamics and vulnerability which characterises that activity. People who make the most effective mentors tend to be those whose dominant quadrant is the **open** area. Why might this be so? Because the mentoring relationship needs to be characterised by authenticity, congruence and transparency in the mentor, qualities only possible if the **open** quadrant is the largest.[2]

PERSONAL REFLECTION (continued)
The ways suggested to reduce the blind quadrant and the hidden quadrant could be covered from time to time with your mentor or supervisor. If you are having difficulties in this, it would be wise to meet with a counsellor.

WORK IN PAIRS
Share at least one aspect of your individual work with your partner.

GROUP WORK
1. In what ways was this exercise helpful?
2. Why is the issue of self-awareness vital for the effective mentor?
3. What reasons do we find here to underscore the importance of having our own mentor and supervisor?
4. What did your learn about self-disclosure?
5. What suggestions are made concerning why some mentors talk too much about themselves?

—✲✲✲—

THE MAIN ROLES OF A MENTOR

There are a number of roles mentors perform. Paul Stanley and Robert Clinton have developed this area extensively, dealing with these roles as 'mentoring types/functions'.[3] It is essentially within this framework that the following has been generated.

Mentoring is not static. Roles keep changing to meet different needs and situations. In the one session a number of roles may be used. In practice, roles overlap one another.

Also, some mentors will be better equipped to fulfil one role more than another and will perform best when operating that way. However, don't be hesitant to enter a weaker role when necessary; quietly pray for wisdom and trust the Holy Spirit to divinely enable you. But know your limitations and be humble enough to confidently admit these and seek out a better-equipped person to help when necessary.

Discovering one's spiritual gifts and taking opportunities to enrich these through reading and various other opportunities will enable the development of effective mentoring functions.

It is difficult to distinguish between each of the roles listed here. Not everyone will be satisfied with the descriptions, as concepts vary according to our temperament, giftedness, training and experience, the context in which we work and other factors.

DISCIPLER

Paul says, '. . . in all things grow up into him who is the head, that is, Christ' (Eph 4:15). 'Disciple' literally means 'learner'. The implication is that discipleship is a process. Indeed, it is a lifetime process – until the day we pass to be with the Lord, we will hopefully continue to grow in our knowledge and experience of Christ. So the role of the mentor as a discipler covers every stage in the life of a disciple of Jesus Christ and indeed undergirds all other mentoring roles.

However, in practice, all too often the church has tended to focus on this role as it relates primarily to a new believer, to help them understand the basics, to become established in their relationship to Christ.

In Chapter 6, p 147, I have outlined what I have found to be helpful in mentoring new believers. One who mentors a new believer need not be a person with great experience and maturity. Indeed, I have used to great effect in this role those who are relatively immature spiritually, but who understand and practise the basics.

SPIRITUAL GUIDE

Paul summarises this role, 'We proclaim him, admonishing and teaching everyone with all wisdom, so that we may present everyone mature in Christ' (Col 1:28). It is essentially about keeping those we help focusing on Christ and keeping their lives open to his grace in the fullest possible way. To keep them 'living in the Spirit and walking in the Spirit' (Gal 5:25).

Effective spiritual guides need to be experienced, Christ-like, wise encouragers with a working knowledge of the Scriptures. They will generally have a long Christian experience they can reflect upon so as to speak with confidence about God's faithfulness amid the mystery and traumas of life. They are aware of their own frailty and utter dependence upon God, so they lead with sensitivity and humility and openly share the lessons they have learnt from their failures as well as their successes.

By asking good questions we facilitate reflection by our mentorees upon their relationship to Christ, their lifestyle in the light of Scripture and their care and concern for others.

I have been enriched by many of the books on **spiritual direction**, particularly that by William A Barry and William J Connolly, who give the following definition of spiritual direction:

'. . . help given by one Christian to another which enables that person to pay attention to God's personal communication to him or her, to respond to this personally communicating God, to grow in intimacy with this God, and to live out the consequences of the relationship. The *focus* of this type of spiritual direction is on experience, not ideas, and specifically on religious experience.'[4]

However, the word 'director' concerns me because some others who teach and write about spiritual direction advocate the need for the 'directee' to take a vow of obedience to the director. While in good mentoring there must be expectations of performance, agreed accountability, the speaking with firmness occasionally, even reprimand and sometimes rescuing, I never see myself as the director, the one who controls, tells, orders and commands. This is not my understanding of the way people learn.

The biblical basis we explore in this book points to the Spirit as the one who directs, motivates, convicts and controls. Some of the New Testament epistles contain rebuke and very strong language, but consistently each writer sees the Spirit as the one who brings about the change that separates us from the natural way of the world as we become attentive to and responsive to the voice of God. The Spirit directs the drama of life; he is the stage manager and the one who enables performance that honours God. It is for this reason that I use the title 'spiritual guide' and not 'spiritual director'. (However, I'm aware of many who use the name 'spiritual director' who fulfil their role according to my understanding of a spiritual guide.)

COACH

Coaching is a response to Paul's challenge 'to equip the saints for the work of ministry' (Eph 4:12). Barnabas is a good biblical example of a coach. He was a godly man, full of the Holy Spirit, one to whom a person could easily relate, who had an effective ministry (Acts 4:36; 11:23,24). He saw the potential in emerging leaders such as Paul, and nurtured their growth and acceptance (Acts 9:27). He knew how to confront (Acts 15:36) and hung in with Paul in the highs and lows of his ministry (Acts 13:2,50). As Paul rose to a more prominent leadership role, Barnabas was not threatened (Acts 11:26; 13:16).

I have many leaders seek me out to help them understand and maximise their ministries. They ask me to comment on their dreams, the way they go about their work, difficulties they meet. They seek my advice and guidance because of my experience as a pastor, educator, writer and administrator.

Coaching relates primarily to:
- provide assistance to another in their ministry;
- unlock their God-given potential;
- enhance their ministry performance;
- increase awareness of the factors which help and hinder performance;
- point out pitfalls in advance;
- process failures;
- identify and seek to remove personal barriers to performance;
- help them take responsibility for their performance;
- enable the development of knowledge and skills appropriate to their specific ministry;
- solve problems and do things better through discussion and guided activity;
- share appropriate knowledge and experience;
- affirm appropriately, encourage, celebrate wins;
- identify with feelings.

Coaching is essentially a hands-on process of helping another succeed in ministry. The artisan/apprentice relationship or the coach of an individual sportsperson or team, are good models. Their roles of teacher, guide, evaluator and encourager, someone to whom another is accountable, illustrate well what is involved.

Academics or theorists without hands-on experience are not qualified to coach. Coaches need the experiential understanding that has grown out of a journey of pain and pleasure, frustration and encouragement, success and failure in the area of their competence.

However coaches will have a good theoretical understanding of principles which undergird and guide their work. This will assist the mentoree to develop an adequate framework and direction for what they do.

Frequently a coach will involve the one they are helping in aspects of their own ministry to not only observe but to give them tasks to perform. The reflection after these times should include evaluation of the coach's performance as well as that of the learner.

Keeping a balance between personal and spiritual growth and ministry performance will be a major concern for a good coach. Spiritual introspection isolates from the cut and thrust of mission, and activism can lead to burnout. The role of the coach needs to be balanced with that of spiritual guide.

COUNSELLOR

There are degrees of counselling, from a word of advice given at a significant moment to an ongoing relationship with the highly trained professional. Wise, godly people have often had a deep impact on another's life and ministry, through even a short conversation. I well remember a sentence or two spoken in brief encounters with mature leaders that continue to guide my actions today. A word from the principal of my theological college to help me to manage my time continually surfaces: 'Learn to choose between the good and the best'. As the proverb goes, 'How good is a timely word' (Prov 15:23).

Pray for wisdom. Along with other friends who are mentors, when I am mentoring I include in my morning prayers the phrase, 'Grant me discernment and wisdom, Lord, that I may speak words as from you in my mentoring today'. Such a prayer is based on the promise in James 1:5, 'If any of you is lacking in wisdom, ask God, who gives to all generously and ungrudgingly, and it will be given you'. Time and again God surprises me with the wise things I say when I'm centred on Christ.

What counsellors do. Counsellors help us get into perspective ourselves, our networks of relationships, our circumstances and our ministry. Asking good questions and listening well are essential for this role. Helping a person think through matters for themselves rather than rushing in with slick advice is an essential skill. Counsellors enable reflection and view issues from a broad perspective so as to unearth causes, to face effects, to identify options, to explore priorities and to link to resources. They help us to own our behaviour and to face and cope with consequences. From this brief description it is obvious that there are limits to the degree of counselling we can give without professional training. It is important to know our limits while not belittling the way the Spirit can use us.

Make referrals. Frequently I refer a mentoree to a professional counsellor so that dysfunctional behaviour can be dealt with in depth. Occasionally the mentoree asks that the counsellor keep me informed of issues being dealt with, so that where appropriate we can think these through from a spiritual perspective.

TEACHER

Helping people learn is integral to most of what a mentor does. In a number of places in this book, learning is dealt with because of its important role. In the section 'Christian Mentoring as Disciplemaking' (Chapter 2, p 17), I explore briefly the teaching dimension of Christ's great commission. 'How Adults Learn' (Chapter 5, p 104) deals with this area more fully. As will be discovered there, people learn both formally and informally.

Formal learning. There will be times when we enter into formal learning situations with our mentorees as we pass on information, have them study a book or other resource, or when they attend a training event. Afterwards we help them explore the authenticity and relevance of this information and experience.

Informal learning. A surprising amount of what we know has been gleaned from life experiences, especially from our relationships. The role of the teacher in experience-based learning is essentially that of enabler, supporting, encouraging the learner in their personal search for meaning from life's experiences.

To assist learning from the review of life and ministry experiences, thoughtful questions can help the learners identify what was happening, consider the thoughts, feelings and actions of all involved and allow them to draw conclusions about the experience. They can then decide what are the options for the way ahead and plan accordingly. Processing of experiences in this way requires of the mentor an unhurried approach, patience, restraint from advice-giving, questioning, listening skills, encouraging the expression of feelings, summarising, planning and enabling the taking of personal responsibility by the learners for their actions. Review of progress and outcomes will ensure that the reflection cycle continues.

SPONSOR

When mentors act as sponsors, they use their position to benefit and protect their mentorees. When I was a young minister, an older leader who held an important position in another denomination, had credibility with his peers and extensive contacts, put my name forward to attend a groundbreaking international conference. He told me that he had observed me over many years and believed I had potential that could be greatly enhanced by participation in this gathering of world leaders. He helped me raise funds, wrote letters supporting my attendance to those to whom I was accountable and introduced me to other participants from Australia. Through the training I received, the resources I became aware of, the world leaders I met and the broad network I formed, that experience greatly enhanced my ministry in the long term. He continued to mentor me, always encouraging, giving wise advice as well as promoting my ministry by introducing me to his networks. That is a good illustration of the sponsoring role.

PASTOR

Pastoring derives its essential nature directly from the person and work of Christ. Servanthood, an essential aspect of pastoring, is best modelled by Christ in every aspect of his life and work: 'I am among you as one who serves' (Luke 22:27).

Jesus washing his disciples' feet in the upper room is an awesome event (John 13:1-17) – the Creator kneeling before the created, washing the dust of travel from their feet, a task the lowliest servant in a house performed. No wonder Peter responded as he did (v 6). Here is a moving demonstration of humility and servanthood. 'I have set you an example that you should do as I have done for you.' (vv 14-16).

Jesus commanded us to 'love as I have loved' (John 15:12). Jesus modelled unselfish, benevolent, outgoing love in his relationship with a wide cross-section of people.

In his epistle, Peter (1 Pet 5:2-4) gives a concise summary of Christ-like pastoring. Peter would never forget his moving dialogue with Jesus after the resurrection, where he learnt that the only genuine motivation for pastors is love for Christ, which will flow through into all their relationships.

Good Christian mentors will be shepherds to their mentorees as they care for them, protect, guide, nourish, comfort, heal and encourage. While they must set limits to the time they can give, there will be a continuing concern that will be evidenced in prayer, occasional phone calls and notes.

MODEL

Much of human behaviour is learnt by the observation of models. Modelling is the greatest form of unconscious learning. Mentorees need models as visual aids, living manifestations of what it means to follow Christ and to continue his ministry – people who demonstrate the art, the skills they need to develop.

Jesus' disciples learnt both formally and informally. While he frequently helped them reflect on everyday experiences, much of what they learnt came from just being with him. They observed his style of living, the way he went about his ministry, his response to the great variety of pressing needs of people, the incredible pressures he experienced because of his popularity and the relentless opposition by the blind religious leaders. They learnt by seeing how he coped with weariness, discouragement, the sense of isolation and rejection. While he taught them how to pray, their greater learning came from observing his need for solitude with his Father on the mountains, in the fields and in the garden.

Probably most of what our mentorees learn from us will be learnt from just being with us, from observing who we are – our being, what we do and the way we do it, our attitudes, our values and our behaviour. They will quickly learn the myth of perfection but hopefully, despite our flawed state, there will be a credibility, a believability, which helps us to be reasonable models of Christian discipleship and ministry.

A few times in his letters, Paul urged his readers to follow his example. His strongest word is in Philippians 4:9, 'Whatever you have learned or received or heard from me, or seen in me – put it into practice'. But again, Jesus is our inspiration here. Christ was

Paul's best model, 'Follow my example as I follow **the example of Christ**' (1 Cor 11:1). John U'Ren, Director of the School of World Mission in Melbourne, frequently asks the question, 'Do they see your priorities and values?'

People will seek us out for mentoring because they have observed the way we minister. Participants in learning events I conduct often ask if they can talk over with me how I lead. Sometimes it results in an ongoing mentoring relationship.

Many are good models of ministry because of long years of faithfully developing their skills doing things well, as well as inspiring others by their commitment and enthusiasm. The less experienced can also be exemplary in their life and work, attracting others who wish to learn from them.

From when I was a new Christian in my late adolescent years, I was encouraged to read biographies and autobiographies of contemporary and historical Christian leaders. Many of these influenced me deeply, becoming important models for me. As mentors, we will encourage the exploring of these models.

Occasionally in our mentoring sessions, when an accessible contemporary Christian leader is discussed, a mentoree may be urged to try to obtain a one-off meeting with that person. If appropriate, that meeting could later be reviewed together. One of my older mentorees was influenced by the writings of a well-known leader from abroad, who lectured frequently in Australia. He wrote to him to try to arrange a meeting during one of his visits. This busy person readily agreed and, after the first meeting, committed himself to meet to converse with him during each of his future visits. The lesson – never pre-judge availability!

ENCOURAGER

> **Mentors must be encouragers. If a mentoree goes away discouraged, we have failed. There should always be a positive and helpful outcome. There will be times when we will speak firmly, even reprimand, but it must always be from a gospel perspective of hope.**

A fanciful story tells of the devil selling off some of his tools of trade to try to balance his budget! Evil spirits came in their hordes to buy. One alert spirit noticed a very impressive tool not on the sale tables. When he approached a supervisor to see if he could purchase it, he was told rather bluntly that it was one of the devil's most effective tools and was definitely not for sale. That was discouragement!

The world is full of discouragers, not all on the devil's payroll! What we need are many more Barnabases (sons and daughters of encouragement). Discouragement is a significant occupational hazard of all followers of Jesus Christ.

Words can have a deep effect upon people – 'Death and life are in the power of the tongue' (Prov 18:21). 'Good words can make an anxious heart glad' (Prov 12:25) and bad words can increase anxiety. James also warns of the power of the tongue to bless or curse (James 3:3-12). Eliphas paid Job a great tribute, 'Your words have kept others on their feet' (Job 4:4, Moffat).

Failure to speak, keeping silent, can also cause discouragement. **Attitudes**, as well as words, also influence the effectiveness of mentoring.

The epistle to the Hebrews instructs us to '**encourage one another daily** . . . so that none of you may be hardened by sin's deceitfulness' (Heb 3:13) and '. . . let us encourage one another – all the more as you see the Day approaching' (Heb 10:25).

Paul's first epistle to the Christians in Thessalonica gives extensive teaching on the need to encourage – to positively influence increased godliness (1 Thess 2:11,12), to inspire courage in the face of trials (1 Thess 3:2,3), to hearten as one hears of the faith and love of others (1 Thess 3:6-10), and to facilitate spiritual development (1 Thess 5:11).

A major source of encouragement, Paul points out, is **Scripture** (1 Thess 4:18, Rom 15:4) with its robust picture of God, the unfolding plan of redemption climaxing in Christ and all the riches of his grace freely offered to us in Christ. Promise after promise is there to encourage as we claim them by faith.

The **ultimate encouragement will be found in God**. That is why so much emphasis is given here to developing and maintaining that relationship – firstly, by the mentor personally, and then as the focus of their work with others.

Encouragement is love expressed. It is an assurance of commitment to another. It gives a sense of support, reduces fear, raises morale and gives confidence. Truth has more chance of affecting transformation in relationships where encouragement is practised. As pointed out in the section 'Walking the Road Together' (Chapter 2, p 34), in this aspect of mentoring we share in the ministry of the Holy Spirit in a very special sense.

STUDY GUIDE

PERSONAL REFLECTION

1. Try to recall the times when a few acted in one or more of these roles to enrich your spiritual life and ministry.
   - In what ways did they do this?
   - What effect did it have upon your life and ministry?
2 'Disciple' literally means 'learner'. What are the ongoing practical implications for us as Christ's disciples?
   - What have been some of the most significant things you have learnt recently, as a 'disciple' of Christ?
   - What feelings accompanied this learning?
   - In what ways have you grown as a result of this?
3. Who models servant-leadership best for you? How?
   - How do you seek to model servant-leadership?
   - What are the implications here for your role as a mentor?
4. What are the advantages of human 'visual aids', 'living demonstrations' in helping others understand and act in Christ-like ways?
   - What people do this for you? How?

GROUP WORK

1. Share your personal reflections.
2. Discuss how Paul's summary of the role of spiritual guide can be put into practice.
3. What is the task of a mentor, untrained in counselling, when faced with this need in their mentoree?
   - How and when will we limit this role?
4. What are some practical modern-day equivalents in your culture to washing another's feet?
5. Discuss 'silence' and 'attitude' as sources of discouragement.

———✳✳✳———

MENTORING STYLES

Many leaders need to make changes to their style if they are to be effective mentors.

FACTORS WHICH DETERMINE STYLE

The style we use in our mentoring will depend essentially upon two factors: our **temperament** and our **perception of mentoring**.

Our **temperament** affects the manner in which we act, feel and think. This, to a large extent, moulds the style of our leadership. Some are naturally autocratic, directive, controlling. Others are passive, laissez-faire, or non-directive. While there is a high degree of permanency here, positive changes can occur as we develop a healthy self-awareness and understand the different styles of leadership, then gain confidence in operating in ways that are appropriate to the needs of each situation, rather than being limited to our natural style.

Our **perception of mentoring** will be affected to a large degree by who we are as a person, but more particularly by our understanding of the purpose of mentoring. One person may see mentoring as being **mentoree-centred**, concerned mainly with his or her personal development and well-being. In contrast, another will see it as **performance-centred**, getting a task done well. In working on performance, mentors may be so knowledgeable, skilled and experienced that they see their role essentially as a 'teller', and 'advice giver, with the 'right answer'. The mentoree is only minimally involved in the process.

Another mentor again may work on improving performance quite differently and act mainly as a facilitator, involving the mentoree in thinking through previous experiences and then planning appropriate action. The mentor acts essentially as a guide, resource and sounding board.

DIRECTIVE AND NON-DIRECTIVE STYLES

Mentoring styles have been described in different ways, going from one extreme to the other. They can be summed up as **directive** or **non-directive**.

The **directive** mentor can often become manipulative, keeping the mentoree in a highly dependent role to satisfy their own needs, usually without realising it.

However, this style of mentoring is not all unhelpful. To push and confront may be useful to maintain staying power when the going gets tough, but is likely eventually to generate resentment.

The **non-directive** mentor acts gently and reassuringly, more like a protective, loving parent than a taskmaster. This is appropriate when a person is bruised by lack of success or by criticism, but may engender future failure through not provoking the person to face reality.

Getting mentorees to think for themselves can mean that they are not able to learn from some aspects of the opposite style, such as availability of the mentor to share knowledge, skills and experience when needed.

FUNCTIONAL STYLE

The ideal mentor is a **functional mentor**, responding to the needs of the mentoree in varying situations. Functional mentors are flexible in their styles. Sometimes they will be directive where there is apathy, confusion or pride, and goals are obscured. When a mentoree is discouraged and lacking in confidence, then the non-directive style will give the necessary gentle reassurance.

Functional mentors are both mentoree- **and** performance-centred. They are holistic in their approach. They keep alert to what is happening in both the life **and** the ministry of the mentoree. They are mentoree-focused, seeking to discern the mentoree's real needs. They increase their charges' focus, self-responsibility and confidence.

However we describe the ideal Christian mentoring style, it must always be sensitive, optimistic and passionate, because it is grounded in the Christian gospel of grace and hope.

GRACE-GIVERS AND TRUTH-TELLERS

Steven Ogne and Thomas Nebel[5] coined the phrases, **'grace-givers'** and **'truth-tellers'** to give us another dimension to our mentoring styles. They briefly define **grace-giving** as 'the art of empowering or encouraging someone in their ministry or their station in life'. **Truth-telling** 'is the art of informing someone about objective reality'. They associate a series of words with each style:

Grace-giver	friend	cheerleader	nice words	suggests	listens	process
Truth-teller	boss	supervisor	hard words	assigns	tells	product

Grace-givers are more concerned with the **process**, whereas **truth-tellers** are more concerned with **product**, what is achieved, reaching a goal, performance.

JESUS' STYLE

Of course, **our ultimate model of style** for Christian mentoring is **our Lord Jesus Christ**. The process was important to him. Truth, faith, hope and love guide the process, but the goal to make disciples and thereby extend God's kingdom and glorify his name should always be kept clearly in view. Jesus' style of balancing grace and truth is our prime model of functional mentoring.

Three incidents in Jesus' ministry clearly illustrate this style of mentoring. Pure grace is movingly demonstrated in Jesus' encounter with the woman taken in adultery and her heartless accusers. The tenderness of his compassion glows so warmly without excusing this moral tragedy. This is grace-giving at its best. But when it was needed, Jesus unhesitatingly operated at the other extreme of the mentoring style continuum as truth-teller, for example, expressing awesome, righteous anger in condemning the teachers of the law and the Pharisees (Matt 23).

At the well near the town of Sychar, Jesus' dialogue with the lonely, rejected Samaritan woman (John 4:4-30) demonstrates a rich balance between grace-giving and truth-telling, resulting in her becoming a convincing witness to him with many coming to faith (vv 39-41).

Jesus knew how to respond to the ever-changing situation of his disciples, always the servant leader but authoritative Lord when appropriate; speaking kind, encouraging words but reprimanding when necessary; listening but knowing when to instruct and cheering on but not controlling. John summed it up so well for us: 'The Word became flesh and made his dwelling among us – full of grace and truth' (John 1:14).

STUDY GUIDE
PERSONAL REFLECTION
1. Below are listed characteristics of different styles of mentoring.
   - Consider each of the *'Mentoring Styles'* (abbreviations: 'non-d' = non-directive; 'dir' = directive; 'fun' = functional), and try to identify which 'characteristic' most nearly applies to each.
   - Seek to determine to what degree each characteristic is true of you personally, placing an 'X' in one or more of the three columns, under *'My Response'* – ('often' 'sometimes' 'never').
   - Place an 'X' in one of the following three columns to indicate which is your natural style, under *'My Style'* (use a '?' if you are uncertain).

CHARACTERISTICS	*MENTORING STYLE*			*MY RESPONSE*			*MY STYLE*		
	non-dir	dir	fun	often	s/times	never	non-dir	dir	fun
Not a good people person									
Fears rejection by person being helped									
Pleasant demeanour									
Talks too much									
A ministry expert									
Hesitant									
An encourager									
Uncomfortable with being direct									
Genuine interest in people									
Low expectations of others									
Controls another's agenda									
Avoids disagreements, conflict									
Lacks self-confidence									
Has sound knowledge, developed skills and wide experience									
Confident about confronting									
Good listener									
Low premium on encouragement									
Fears not succeeding									
Direct – comes to the point									

2. How do you feel about what you learnt about yourself in the above exercise?
   - Where do you need to make changes to your style?
3. What changes, if any, do you need to make to increase your ability as both a grace-giver and a truth-teller?
4. Who could help you make any changes that you may now find necessary?
   - When will you approach them?

GROUP WORK
1. Share your individual work in pairs.
2. Another word for functional leadership is *maieutic*. It comes from the Greek word *maieuomai* meaning 'serve as a midwife' (*maia* = midwife).
   - Discuss mentoring as being midwives of the Holy Spirit, in enabling the Christian life to be a series of new beginnings for our mentorees or our co-mentors.
3. Discuss Jesus' role as grace-giver and truth-teller in the two instances given.
   - Can you think of further instances in Christ's ministry?
   - Think of some actual or imagined situations in which Jesus' style would have improved your leadership or mentoring.
4. The group may want to role play an incident from Jesus' ministry or another aspect of the styles dealt with.

———✳✳✳———

OUR PERSONAL MENTORING RESOURCES
People will seek us out to draw upon various aspects of our knowledge, experience, competence, giftedness, skills, etc. Some will want to focus on only one aspect of our personal resources to meet their present needs; others will want to benefit from most of what we have to offer.

> **Who you are in Christ, the first entry listed below, is the essential resource. Without this resource, none of us can effectively undertake Christian mentoring. Our experiences of Christ will vary and so will our spirituality, but the one constant is that we have a personal, living relationship with him.**

Good negotiation in the first meeting will clarify the focus of the mentoring. However, as the relationship develops, other resources may be sought from the mentor. No one mentor has all the resources needed for effective Christian living and ministry. Indeed, some of the most effective mentors may appear to be strong in only a few areas. It is important that mentors recognise their limitations and act as a bridge to other specialist resources.

Here are some of our possible resources:
• Who you are in Christ
• Who you are as a person
• Your spiritual gifts
• Your knowledge and understanding of the Scriptures
• The skills you have developed
• Life experiences
• Ministry experiences
• Just being a good listener
• Your ability to encourage
• Your availability
• Your network of relationships
• Your knowledge of available resources
• Your influence within systems and organisations (for sponsoring).

While I seek to encourage those hesitant to consider entering into this ministry of mentoring, I must indicate that not all people are suitable. The first item listed above is basic, but others are also most important. For example, if you are a very poor listener, a compulsive talker, too busy or find it difficult to keep confidences, there may be other aspects of ministry for you, but not mentoring.

STUDY GUIDE

PERSONAL REFLECTION

Try to identify something of what you have to offer to others.

- **Who you are in Christ.** What differences has Christ made to your life? What does your relationship to him mean to you in practical terms each day? In what ways has he affected the way you relate to others (not just your friends)?
- **Who you are as a person.** List words which people use to describe you when they affirm you, eg positive, caring, reliable, sensitive, generous, etc.
- **Spiritual gifts.** Dr Bob Hillman has identified twenty-seven spiritual gifts listed in the New Testament[6]:
  Speaking Gifts: apostle, prophet, evangelist, teacher, pastor, exhortation, the word of wisdom, the word of knowledge, discernment, missionary, courage (martyrdom), speaking in tongues, interpretation of tongues.
  Serving Gifts: service, mercy, helping, assistance, voluntary poverty, giving, leadership, faith, administration, celibacy, hospitality, intercession, healing, miracles and exorcism.
  Scripture passages dealing with these include: 1 Cor 12:1-13:13; Rom 12:1-8; Eph 4:7-13. (See Gordon D Fee's excellent discussion of the gifts in the Corinthian context in the New International Commentary on the New Testament: *The First Epistle to the Corinthians*, Grand Rapids, Eerdmans, 1987.) Which of these are your gifts? Which are your strongest?

  (If you are uncertain about your spiritual gifts, study the above passages using a reliable commentary, then read a good book about spiritual gifts).

  Ask other Christian friends what they think your gifts may be.

  Reflect on what you enjoy doing most and in which you are most effective. This is a good indicator.

  Use one of the following spiritual gift tests to confirm your gifts. One test is published by Church Growth Institute, PO Box 4404, Lynchburg, VA, 24502. Trenton Spiritual Gifts Analysis (published by the Charles E Fuller Institute of

Evangelism and Church Growth, PO Box 91990, Pasadena, California 91109-1990) is another such test.

- **Knowledge and understanding of the Scriptures.** How well do you know the Scriptures? What have you done to improve your knowledge?
- **Skills you have developed.** What do you do well?
- **Life experiences.** Review your life to date by selecting some key events, high and low points. What was the significant learning for you in some of these?
- **Ministry experiences.** Treat this in the same way as you did **Life experiences**.
- **Being a good listener.** Do you listen well or do you talk over people while they are talking? Do you keep interjecting with your own story while the focus should be on the others, or do you listen well in the ways outlined in Chapter 5, p 129?
- **Ability to encourage.** Do people give you feedback telling you how you encouraged them and others?
- **Availability.** Do you find it easy to make yourself available to others when they need you? Do your life commitments prevent you being as available as you would like to be? Despite, say, home or work commitments, do you make yourself readily accessible by means of the phone or e-mail?
- **Network of relationships.** Seek to identify your networks in your church, with other denominations, in the community, special interest groups, etc.
- **Knowledge of available resources.** Do you browse through Christian bookshops regularly? Are you a good reader? Do you talk to others about appropriate resources for your own or others' needs?
- **Influence within systems and organisations (for sponsoring):** Do you hold leadership positions in these? Of what committees are you a member? How many influential leaders do you know well?

What you have to offer
Now try to identify those areas that are your strengths.
- Why did you choose these?
- In what ways would a mentoree benefit from these?

> **GROUP WORK**
> **In pairs**
> • If your partner knows you well, begin by asking them what they think your strengths are in some of these areas.
> • Share as much of your above work as you feel able and discuss aspects of this.

———✳✳✳———

BEGINNING AS A MENTOR

As stated at the commencement of this book, mentoring is a very significant role every Christian disciple can fulfil (irrespective of age or experience. It is not restricted to 'giants of the faith'. The basic requirement is a living relationship with God, and an ability to listen and respond sensitively. If this is true of you, you can be God's agent in enriching another person's life.

Mentoring operates at different levels. The more knowledgeable, experienced and skilled a person, the deeper the level at which they will work. However, much great work in the kingdom of God is done not by the obvious mentors but by people we normally overlook for this role. Each and every member of Christ's body has a distinct function to perform and is gifted accordingly (1 Cor 12:7; Eph 4:7). You may want to re-read 1 Cor 1:26-31.

TO HELP YOU BEGIN

> **STUDY GUIDE**
>
> *PERSONAL REFLECTION*
> **Pray:** Mentoring, as with all service in the name of Christ, is an extension of Christ's ministry. It is God, the Holy Spirit, who equips and empowers us (Eph 3:16; 1 Cor 2:4; Rom 15:13; Acts 1:8, 4:31) and guides us in performing this work (Acts 8:29, 16:6,7; Rom 8:14). So begin by praying for the Holy Spirit's guidance in preparing yourself and in finding those with whom God wants you to work. Here could be the starting point for you in becoming a most useful mentor.
> • Who could you ask to pray for you in this regard?
> • When will you approach them?

Reflect on past experiences: This will help you recognise how God has already been using you in supporting others.

(a) Help in your journey: Think about people who helped you in significant ways, especially when there were new beginnings and critical times during your:

Childhood, adolescence, young adulthood, adulthood

Journey in faith – discipleship

Education and work

Relationships – friendships, marriage, family

Sickness, death

- List some of these important events and next to each the names of those who helped you.
- In what ways did these people help you, why was it helpful and how did it make you feel?
- If support was lacking at these vital times, what help would you have appreciated?

Write what becomes clear to you generally from this reflection.

(b) Help you have given to others: Think of times when you have provided support for others during key events in their lives.

- What did you do? How did it help?
- How did you feel about it?
- What was their response?

Identifying potential mentorees

It will be helpful to refer to the **life stages** mentioned in Chapter 6 under 'Strategies for Other Situations', p 160, before undertaking the following:

Using the themes which provided a framework for your thinking in the last section (childhood, etc), think of one or more people who are in new stages of their development or experiencing difficulties. Could you provide guidance, encouragement and practical support for them?

- What actions could you take?
- From whom could you seek advice to ensure your anticipated actions are appropriate?
- How will you approach a potential mentoree?
- When will you do this?

FURTHER SUGGESTIONS
Here are some things I have found helpful for making connections with potential mentorees.

Keep alert to unspoken cries for help. In casual conversations there are many cries for help in chance indirect remarks and emotional responses. Use your active listening skills to check whether you are hearing what the person is really saying and feeling.

Issue open-ended invitations. After an apparent emerging leader impresses me, or I become aware of people facing new challenges or crises, I simply say, 'If ever you think I can help, don't hesitate to contact me'. I am surprised at the number taking me up on this offer, so I don't make it lightly.

Recognise approaches from potential mentorees. See 'Finding a Mentor' in Chapter 7, p 175. Some will approach you for help in a very tentative manner, especially if they think you are busy. Others will be quite shy about making themselves vulnerable. In such cases, the real messages they are trying to convey may be difficult to recognise. Again, your active listening skills will help.

Don't be quick to commit yourself. Suggest that you meet together. Talk about the possibility of working together then see how each of you feels.

[1] *With Open Hands*, Henri J M Nouwen, Ave Maria Press, Notre Dame, 1972 [1995].
[2] This section is contributed by Greg and Meryem Brown, **synergia** *human resource consultants*, PO Box 23, Kippa-ring, QLD 4021.
[3] *Connecting*, Paul D Stanley and J Robert Clinton, Navpress, 1992
[4] *The Practice of Spiritual Direction*, William A Barry and William J Connolly, Harper & Row, 1982
[5] *Empowering Leaders through Coaching*, Stephen L Ogne & Thomas P Nebel, Direction Ministry Resources, 1995
[6] *27 Spiritual Gifts*, Robert Hillman, JBCE, Melbourne, 1990

CHAPTER 5

TOOLS AND SKILLS FOR MENTORING

THE CRUCIAL ROLE OF PRAYER

As I write this, in front of me on my desk is a photo of a clay sculpture by the German Erdmann Hinz, who died while still an adolescent, called 'The Praying Beggar'. This picture has captivated me since I came across it some years ago. Most mornings as I commence my prayers, I focus on this stooped figure with expectant uplifted face and large, empty, extended hands. I recall the opening words of Jesus' Sermon on the Mount: 'Blessed are the poor in spirit for theirs is the kingdom of God' (Matt 5:3). I come with a sense of abject spiritual poverty into the presence of my generous heavenly Father, to open myself anew to receive all the grace he has for me for that day.

I am driven to wait on God because of my great sense of helplessness as I anticipate the tremendous privilege and awesome responsibility of being a bearer of the life-transforming gospel of Christ – a bridge between needy human beings and God's superabundant undeserved kindness.

I pray regularly because of my acute awareness of how unworthy and ill-equipped I am to handle the sacred – to minister to souls whose eternal destiny could be influenced by the reality or otherwise of my relationship to God.

THE NEED FOR PRAYER SUPPORT

I am also committed to the **power of collective prayer**. The greatest proof of this to me is Pentecost, where the eternal church of Christ was born at a prayer meeting. As a young minister, I learnt to regularly ask my congregation to pray for me. I continued to do this as I moved around Australia and overseas, leading training events.

I have over four hundred prayer partners who have committed themselves to pray for me daily, but not until eternity will I know the full extent of those who uplift me before the throne of grace regularly. I regularly send my prayer partners items for intercession and thanksgiving.

I have also learnt to use small prayer chains, activated by a phone call or a note sent by mail or e-mail, for the more immediate needs which arise in between the prayer notes I send to my larger group of prayer partners.

I believe in the gift of intercession. Some people are specially endowed by the Holy Spirit to intercede regularly with strong faith to great effect. With my two intercessors, I share the more intimate aspects of my life and ministry, so I am very much aware of the power of their prayers.

If what I do one-to-one and in large groups appears to be effective, I have no hesitation in attributing it not primarily to my skills, my experience or who I am, but essentially to the power of the Holy Spirit being released through the ministry of prayer.

After addressing my mentoree's personal prayer life I encourage them to enlist others to pray for them. This they can do in a general way by asking those they lead, or are close to, to pray for them. More specifically I encourage them to develop a prayer base similar to that outlined above. To begin this, I advise that they seek out at least one person who will act as their personal intercessor. This person should be someone who believes in them, encourages them, can be trusted completely and with a gift of intercession. The intercessor should receive regular detailed updates of each week's program along with specific personal and ministry needs. They should be contacted immediately whenever unexpected challenges or crises arise. Answers to their prayers should also be shared as a means of encouragement.

Regarding a mentoree's regular personal prayer, I try not to be legalistic or have unrealistic expectations in the short term as they develop a prayer base, but would hesitate to continue as their mentor if they failed to take the need for prayer seriously.

PRAYER WITH MENTOREES

Prayer has a significant place in my mentoring sessions. I pray beforehand for wisdom and grace, recalling the specific needs of my mentorees. During the session we may occasionally pray to celebrate something or to address a deep need. We never conclude without prayer to lift up to God the matters discussed. I frequently contact my mentorees between sessions, often only to pray with them. My needs as a mentor are also included in my personal prayers of intercession.

THE NEED FOR PRAYER IN EFFECTIVE MENTORING

Prayer is the greatest need today in Christian service and unfortunately the most neglected. The most important thing I can teach a Christian mentor is to undergird their ministry with prayer. Unless they do this, regardless of how skilled a mentor they are, there will seldom be any lasting value in what they achieve for the kingdom of God and the glory of Christ's name. **Personal spirituality and mission, prayer and work, faith and action, withdrawal and participation belong together.**

We need to keep coming back to that saying of Jesus, 'Without me you can do nothing'. In a sense, this is not quite true, for we can do a lot of things without Jesus, but unfortunately they won't count for eternity. As the old hymn goes,

> 'Nothing in my hand I bring,
> simply to your cross I cling:
> naked, come to you for dress,
> helpless, look to you for grace . . .'

Not only do we, as mentors, need to learn this vital lesson but it should be a special focus in our time with those we are seeking to serve in this unique ministry. Prayer is crucial in all we do in the name of our Lord Jesus Christ.

STUDY GUIDE

PERSONAL REFLECTION

1. How do you respond to the opening paragraphs of this chapter.
2. What are some of the significant answers you have had to prayer?
3. Look up these promises concerning prayer and choose one that gets your attention, noting the way in which it does: Exod 33:17; Ps 10:17; Ps 37:4; Isa 65:24; Zech 10:2; Matt 18:19; Mark 11:24,25; Luke 11:13; John 16:23,24; Rom 8:26; Rom 10:12; Jas 1:5.
4. 'Teach us to pray', the disciples said to Jesus. If you had been present then, what help would you have sought from Jesus concerning prayer?
   - Bring to the group a book that has helped you to pray (if you have one).
5. How aware are you of the prayers of others?
6. Who could you ask to pray for you regularly?
   - Make a list of a few things for which you would value prayer.
   - For what answers to prayer can you genuinely be thankful?

(These are the kind of items you will give to your prayer partners on a regular basis. Bring these items on a piece of paper to the small group meeting to use in a prayer segment.)

GROUP EXPERIENCE

1. Begin with a time of praise centred on God's sovereignty, faithfulness and willingness to hear our prayers.
2. In pairs: Exchange the items for prayer you each listed under 6 above. Briefly elaborate on them. Pray together for five minutes.
3. Share your responses to the opening paragraph of this chapter.
   - Follow with a period of open prayer as a group, issuing specifically from this joint reflection.
4. Share your Scripture verses and a significant answer to prayer (2 and 3) under Personal Reflection.

5. Share your response to 4 under Personal Reflection.
   - What are some resources that could meet some of the needs expressed?
   - What plans could you make as a group to improve your prayer life?
6. Pray together for:
   - Those you are hoping to mentor.
   - The mentoring scheme you may be establishing in your church.
   - A couple of items from the daily news which need prayer.
7. Close with a time of praise followed by a blessing.

USING THE BIBLE – OUR PRIME MENTORING RESOURCE

Eugene Petersen has some pertinent things to say about the important place of the New Testament in authentic spirituality. 'Christians have a great gift to offer the world in all matters of spirituality. It is our New Testament. There is nothing quite like it. It is the greatest gift we can provide for people who are fed up with the hand-to-mouth existence of mere appetite. It is the perfect gift for people who are bored with the head-trip existence of mere intellect. It is the exactly right gift for people who have gone stale on second-hand religion.

'Meanwhile Christians have in their keeping this document, *The New Testament*, that has all the marks of the real thing. They have been reading and meditating on it for nearly two thousand years. Every kind and sort of Christian has tested it against every kind and sort of circumstance and condition of living and stood up to give witness to its validity. Tested against the reality of actual lives, it turns out to be not another of many "guesses" about spirituality, but spirituality itself. Instead of reading *about* spirituality, getting careful definitions or elaborate descriptions of it, we come upon spirituality in action. Reading the New Testament, we are immersed in the intricate tangle of human life as it is entered, addressed, confronted, saved, healed and blessed by the living God – God's Spirit breathed into human lives. Spirituality.

'It is the great responsibility and privilege of Christians today to place this proven and essential source document on spirituality in the hands of those who are bewilderingly searching through a welter of spiritualities for something authentic, something true.'[1]

DEVELOP SKILLS IN USING THE BIBLE

Authentic Christian mentoring will keep referring back to the Bible as our 'final authority in all matters of faith'. This is not a popular concept in our post-modern world but the alternative is confusion, where everybody claims they have a franchise on spiritual truth.

A Christian mentor will seek to have a working knowledge of the Bible. Ignorance of biblical truth or inability to apply the Scriptures to life situations greatly limits the effectiveness of Christian mentoring. Many mentors will have had the privilege of formal training in Bible and theology, others without this training will have developed skills in using the Bible through years of experience in reading and studying the Bible informally. Those without this background should be encouraged to improve their knowledge and understanding through involvement in the many training opportunities available today. Christian bookshops abound with books to improve our skills in handling the Bible adequately.

HELP MENTOREES TO TAKE THE BIBLE SERIOUSLY

In our mentoring we will not only seek to help our mentorees know what the Bible says, but encourage them to take it seriously and put it into practice.

James wisely says, 'For if any are hearers of the word and not doers, they are like those who look at themselves in a mirror . . . but those who look into the perfect law, the law of liberty, and persevere, being not hearers who forget but doers who act – they will be blessed in their doing' (Jas 1:23,25).

As Dietrich Bonhoeffer says, 'It is never sufficient simply to have read God's word. It must penetrate deep within us, dwell in us like the Holy of Holies in the Sanctuary, so that we do not sin in thought, word or deed.

'Just knowing Scripture does not mean that it will change us or automatically prevent us from doing wrong. Scripture must be believed, must come alive for us as being important and relevant, and must be acted upon if it is to be a power for good in our lives. The power of Scripture lies in its ability to give the wanderer direction; the disillusioned, hope; the seeker, answers; the discouraged, comfort; and provide us with the words that reflect God's heart and purpose. **God's word must become part of the way we think if it is to direct us.**'[2]

There are a number of books which help relate scriptural teaching to life situations. Some, such as *Topical Analysis of the Bible*,[3] are very comprehensive reference books, but one which is practical and in a handy, easy-to-use form is the *Lion Concise Book of Bible Quotations*.[4] It can be easily carried in a pocket or purse to a mentoring session or kept by the phone. It contains what the Bible says about behaviour, attitudes and values. Scriptural references to faith, love, suffering, prayer and a host of other subjects are listed.

Asking questions such as 'What persons and situations would you relate to differently if you took this seriously?' or 'What changes would this make in your attitudes and behaviour if you acted on this?' help earth the Scriptures in our lives.

STUDY GUIDE
PERSONAL REFLECTION
1. How receptive are you to allowing others to apply the 'one another' passages to your life?
   - Grade your receptivity by placing a 'tick' in the appropriate columns:

	not at all	*a little*	*much*	*very much*
Carry your burdens (Gal 6:1,2)				
Build you up in Christ (1 Thess 5:11)				
Protect you from sin (Heb 3:12-14)				
Listen to your confession and pray for you (James 5:16)				
Love you (John 13:34,35; 1 John 3:11)				

- Can you think of reasons why you placed ticks in the left-hand columns?
- Who could help you in this?
2. In what ways can you identify with the points Eugene Peterson makes at the beginning of this section about people's search for an authentic spirituality? (Note expressions such as 'mere appetite', 'mere intellect', 'second-hand religion', 'guesses about spirituality'.) How has the New Testament had 'all the marks of the real thing' for you?
3. Part of this section encourages us to put into practice what the Bible says.
   - Take a verse of the New Testament (eg Phil 4:6,7) and write it in your own words – as you would say it in a letter to a friend. Don't embellish it – keep it simple, but make its meaning clear.
   - Now ask these questions of this passage and record your answers: If I really took this seriously, in what ways would I be different? What relationships and situations would be affected? In what ways?

GROUP WORK
In pairs:
- Share any of your response to 1 and follow this with prayer for each other.

As a group:
- Share responses to the Peterson quote.
- In turn, let each person give their own paraphrase of the Scripture passage and responses to the questions. (Let **all** contribute **before** there is any discussion.)
- In what ways can you improve your understanding of the Bible?

—✳✳✳—

HOW ADULTS LEARN
Each learner is different. There is no one way to learn. There are many different styles of learning. People learn in different ways. Some learn best by observing how another person does something, then try it themselves until they have perfected the activity or

become proficient through further watching and inquiry. Others learn best by listening, quickly grasping what is said and then applying their understanding. Others need visual presentations to accompany a verbal presentation. Reading is another way some learn best, while interacting in a small group provides the stimulation others need.

Mentors need to discover which way their mentorees learn best, in order to maximise the mentoring experience. Some will already be well aware of their ideal learning style, while others will need help in thinking through how they have previously gained information and skills. If the mentor is unable to adapt, this may mean the mentor/mentoree match may not be appropriate.

EXPERIENCE-BASED LEARNING

Informal learning usually takes place when people are least aware that they are gathering information and developing skills. This is one of the most powerful ways people learn. People learn in many different situations. Every area and circumstance of life provides an environment for learning: our homes, our workplaces, where we worship, when and where we serve and care for others, our leisure activities, sickness and health, joy and sorrow, success and failure.

One of the great benefits of small groups is that in the interaction during discussions and the sharing of life experiences, people have the opportunity to grow in knowledge and understanding.

As people perform activities they find ways of doing things better. It may or may not be recognised as learning at the time, but in retrospect is seen as significant. Creative people who are encouraged to think, reflect and experiment, can make major contributions to the improvement of the way things are done.

Experience-based learning involves a conscious effort to process and learn from experiences in which we have been involved. This can be done on one's own, but often another person or a small group is involved.

The apprenticeship model used in training tradespeople is an excellent example. While training is received in an educational institution, the major component of learning takes place in the workplace with a qualified person. The learner observes and questions. Competency is developed as tasks are undertaken under supervision. Reflection is involved, leading to increased understanding and confidence.

This is the most common form used by Jesus in training and equipping his disciples. He modelled what he wanted them to learn. Daily the disciples observed Jesus' lifestyle, seeing the way he worked, sharing his thoughts. He trusted them with aspects of his ministry, reviewing with them their successes and failures.

This form of learning is essentially what takes place in good mentoring.

THE IMPORTANT ROLE OF REFLECTION

Reflection helps turn experience into learning. It is the central factor in experience-based learning. It is a process in which we can revisit our experiences, seek to analyse what was happening, to identify behaviour, ideas and feelings. The positive aspects of these are affirmed as useful for future experience and ways explored to remove the negative aspects. The new perspectives on specific past experiences can lead to discovery of alternate ways to enable future experiences in similar situations to be more effective.

The three basic questions to help reflection are: 'What happened?' 'What does it mean?' and 'What can I do?'

In mentoring, our aim is to produce reflective disciples of Christ.

MENTORING AS EXPERIENCE-BASED LEARNING

Mentoring provides an ideal situation for learning by experience. In experience-based learning, mentorees are enabled to analyse their past and current experiences by reflecting and evaluating, in order to make sense of them in a way that will help them grow and become more effective in their future actions. The focus is upon the mentoree, who is helped by the mentor to fully participate in the process.

David Kolb, the American experiential learning theorist, developed Kurt Lewin's experiential learning cycle, which is a useful way of explaining Kolb's view that learning is a continuous process, grounded in experience. To learn from experience we need to take time to reflect on a specific action, thinking about it and making sense of it, then planning ways of acting more effectively in the future.

In this form of learning, the mentoree is supported on a journey of discovery rather than acting as a passive participant in a didactic learning situation or listening to a 'teller'. This mode of learning is more likely to produce change in attitudes, values and behaviour than formal learning.

The mentor needs skill in helping the mentoree to reflect and evaluate. The ability to ask good questions and listen is primary in making it easier for quality reflection to occur, thus creating significant learning outcomes.

Questions for reflection: Some questions to use in the reflection/evaluation process relating to a specific experience could include:

- What was your purpose?
- How did you prepare?
- What went well/not so well?
- What feelings did you identify in yourself and others?
- Which of the feelings were unhelpful?
- In what ways can these obstructive feelings be removed in future similar experiences?
- What were the positive feelings?
- How can these positive feelings be utilised in the future?
- What did you learn about yourself?
- What did you learn about your ministry?
- What did you learn about 'you in ministry'?
- What do you think Jesus would do in a similar situation?
- What does Scripture have to say that is relevant here?
- What did you learn about God in this experience?
- What would you do the same in future?
- What would you do differently?
    (You may need to explore options and select the most appropriate – brainstorming could be helpful)
- What/who could hinder or block you in doing things differently? How will you handle this?

- What/who could be of help?

  How and when will you enlist this help?

In this mode of learning, the mentor acts as a facilitator. While the mentor will be a provider of information, this will be given at an appropriate point in the reflection/planning process without dominating or diverting the flow of the mentoree's self-discovery.

Learning from experience necessitates the development of good rapport between the mentor as the facilitator and the mentoree as the learner. The relational dimension is central to its effectiveness. Empathy, active listening, trust, respect for boundaries and lack of manipulation or coercion are essential.

SPECIAL EXPERIENCES FOR REFLECTION

Sometimes it will be appropriate to organise special experiences for the mentoree for later reflection. It is common practice in vocational and professional education to use many forms of experience-based learning. Some that are suitable for a mentoring situation are case studies, journalling, interviews, field trips, critical incident reports, action research, on-the-job training and problem-based learning. Journalling is dealt with in the next section but here is a brief explanation of a few of the more commonly used of these.

A case study is an account of a factual or made-up situation which mentorees may face in their life or work. These can be prepared by the mentor or located in an article, book or video.

Questions are the key to making good use of the case study. These could include:

- What are you thinking/feeling?
- In what ways is this situation similar to your own?
- In what ways is it different?
- What are the main issues here?
- Who are the key players and in what ways do they contribute, either positively or negatively?
- What is relevant to your own life and ministry?

Interviews and field trips. A competent person or a situation in an area of interest to your mentoree could be observed and/or worked with/in and then reflected upon. Help may be needed to set up this experience. Ensure there is adequate preparation – talk about the background of the person and their areas of competency. Enable identification of what information is to be sought. The experience is followed up by discussion in a mentoring session of what was learnt and its relevance.

A critical incident report is similar to a case study, but is limited to a moment in a mentor's life or work that parallels that of their mentoree. For example it could be an incident of violent outrage expressed in a committee meeting to another member. The report on the imagined or actual situation would need to provide background on those directly involved, the leadership and other members of the committee.

Discussion of this report could focus on the mentoree's most appropriate feelings and actions if he/she was the 'victim', chairperson or an uninvolved member of the committee.

This form of learning needs to be closely linked to situations the mentorees may encounter from time to time. These enable them to discover their people-skills, self-awareness, ability to cope with stress, etc.

Some such reports should cover how to cope with success and also with difficult situations, such as failure and conflict.

BRAINSTORMING is suggested above and in other sections of this book. To do this effectively, two or more people should say whatever comes into their minds relative to the issue. These should be written down quickly without comment or discussion. Only when all ideas have been exhausted should the ideas be evaluated. Those deemed inappropriate should be crossed out and the others prioritised, until one or a few are adopted or seen as good possibilities.

Further reading on experience-based learning
J Dewey, *Experience and Education*, New York, Collier Books, 1938.
P Freire, *Pedagogy of the Oppressed*, New York, The Seabury Press, 1973.
D Kolb, *Experiential Learning: Experience as the Source of Learning and Development*, Englewood Cliffs, NJ, Prentice Hall, 1984.

The Australian Consortium of Experiential Education (ACEE) provides a network for practitioners of experiential learning and has been instrumental in providing a professional base for developing innovative activities in the EBL field. Its newly revised journal, the *Australian Journal of Experiential Learning*, contains both theoretical and practical contributions, and also acts as a clearing house for Australian and international experiential learning activities.

STUDY GUIDE
PERSONAL REFLECTION
1. In what way do you think you learn best? What learning experiences support this view?
2. Make brief notes of two experiences you had in ministering to others (one which went well, one not so well) and use a few of the Questions for Reflection to help you think it through, making notes of your answers.

GROUP WORK
1. In groups of three or four, share your responses to 1 and 2 above. There will probably not be enough time for all to give full details of their work, so keep to general responses.
2. Why is experience-based learning the best way to learn in a mentoring situation?
3. Socrates taught his students by asking questions – he seems to have seldom, if ever, given answers.
   What are the advantages and disadvantages of this style of learning?
4. Study the case study and/or a critical incident report that your trainer has prepared for the group.

—✳✳✳—

JOURNALLING
'Journal writing is reflective writing.'[5] It enables us to ponder our varied experiences in order to learn from them so we may grow personally and spiritually and our ministry become more credible.

Self-knowledge leads to humility, which is the key to swing wide the door of our lives to God's love.

Journalling introduces the important dimension of autobiography into learning experiences, personalising the learning, strengthening the ownership of the experience and the awareness of relevance for future action.

Journalling is an important tool in the mentoring process, enabling reflection and aiding the mentor in questioning and discussion. In the mentoring context it presents a number of possibilities.

As stated in the previous section, adults learn in different ways. The same style of learning does not suit everyone. This must be kept in mind when considering journalling. Mentorees will need to discover in what ways journalling is appropriate for them. Some take to it like ducks to water, others will flounder. Some will enjoy writing copious notes almost daily, while others will find jotting down a few notes irregularly is appropriate.

The availability of sufficient time in a busy daily schedule is another important factor. Indeed, there will be those for whom regular reflection with their mentor, using good reflective questions, will be sufficient.

Writing a regular, daily journal is not my style. However, I value my journal writing and do it as often as possible. My retreat days and vacations are when I do some of my best journalling.

Some of my most effective journalling is done when I am seeking guidance on an important issue for myself, or for someone I am helping. Then I journal quite regularly for a period, to ensure I don't miss some leads from my reading of Scripture, listening in prayer, 'nudges of the Spirit' (the hunches I get), snippets from informal conversations, the wise advice of mature friends, my feelings and circumstances.

Making rigid requirements for those who do not find reflective writing their style is akin to making a left-handed person write with their right hand.

JOURNALLING IN THE MENTORING PROCESS

Mentors frequently encourage their mentorees to journal the aspects of their life and ministry they are dealing with in the mentoring sessions. Issues to be raised with the mentor are recorded to ensure they are not overlooked and insights gained during the session noted, along with matters to be explored further.

Work to be undertaken between sessions is also listed along with any long- or short-term goals. Work done in connection with these assignments is also noted in the journal, together with reflection on significant experiences.

Mentors also make brief notes of some of the above, especially the latter aspects. This builds a basis for accountability and for occasional reviews of overall progress and evaluation.

I go through my notes prior to a mentoring session to refresh my memory and give thought to appropriate questions and possible direction for the time together.

JOURNALLING IN GENERAL

We deal here with the more common use of journalling. It is a most useful practice, encouraging attention to detail in a wide range of experiences and requiring careful analysis and reflection on the thoughts, feelings and actions comprising these experiences.

Mentors often incorporate this form of journalling into their work with their mentorees. The privacy dimension needs to be maintained, so there should be no coercion to share any aspect. Just the fact that the journal is being kept is sufficient in most cases.

Sometimes in peer mentoring by mutual agreement, some or all aspects are shared openly with each other.

Jana Rea introduces us to this common form of journalling:
'Journals are a record or landmark in the redemption process. They keep us accountable on a daily basis, expectant and watchful for redemptive possibilities in each new day.

'And so our journal will contain a blend of discovery. It is a safe place to do exploration, shed our misconceptions, reclaim our lost or forgotten parts, recover the fragments that living makes of us at times, and cultivate the gift of new life. In this way, journal writing becomes a viable prayer form, and our journal our own book of psalms. In the privacy of personal reflection, insights are received, confessions are offered, progress is noted. Journal writing fosters a careful attention to our soul's condition, and we are better for the tending.

'Inner questions often emerge in the process. A good question always has a prodding quality that is invaluable to our faith. And a good journal tracks these questions even if they remain unanswered for years.'[6]

HINTS FOR KEEPING A JOURNAL

Here are some suggestions for journal writing which apply especially to the second form of mentoring outlined above, but also to the first.

Decide upon your focus: Journal writing can cover all areas of our personal and spiritual life and service, or it can concentrate on one or more. Here are just a few possibilities:

- **Self-awareness.** Writing to think through attitudes and values, behaviour, feelings and our significant experiences.
- **Relationships.** Processing our varied experiences with people.
- **Our spirituality.** Noting the ways God gets our attention, especially in our reading of the Bible, and also other Christian books. Recording our prayers, including our struggles with God, along with answers received.
- **Ministry.** Reflection on our motives, passions, challenges, difficulties, disappointments, joys and victories.

Pray: Pause to centre your thoughts, and pray initially. Pray for help to understand and respond to what God might show you.

Reflect: Journalling as 'reflective writing' requires that we endeavour to look objectively at ourselves and our experiences. It involves 'self observation' and 'self questioning'.

- Questions which help us in our initial reflection on life experiences are 'What happened?', 'What was helpful and unhelpful?', 'How did I feel?'
- When reflecting on your reading of the Bible, use questions such as these suggested to readers of Scripture Union's Daily Bread guide: What does the passage say to me? Is there a promise, a command, an example, a warning?
  What do I discover about God the Father and creator, the Lord Jesus or the Holy Spirit?
  What do I learn about people and their relationship with God or each other?

Let it flow: Just write what comes to mind without concern about its literary quality or analysis. Write spontaneously but thoughtfully.

Tell it like it is: This is your private record, so be frank and honest about all your certainties and questions, your successes and failures, your struggles and victories, your fears, doubts and assurances.

Use 'I' language: Put everything in the first person singular – 'I', 'me', 'mine', etc.

Record your actual feelings, not your ideal feelings. Don't repress them. Don't hide negative feelings towards God. He already knows them, so own them. Include both negative and positive feelings – warmth and pleasure, anger and fear, thankfulness and disappointment, joy and sorrow.

Be patient: Most people find it takes time to develop the freedom to write spontaneously and honestly.

Do it regularly: Try to develop a regular routine. However, we are all different. Some people find no difficulty journalling daily, while others do it weekly or less regularly. Some may need to develop a discipline in this regard. However, it should never be unrealistic or stressful.

Search for meaning in what you have written: Question, analyse, face realities, explore options. If you have regular retreat days, this is an ideal time to reflect over a broader area of your journalling. Some keep a separate journal especially for recording the work done in their retreat days.

Plan action: Inward reflections need to be expressed in performance. Seeking of forgiveness from God may lead to the need of healing of a relationship. The commitment to action needs to be prompt, but the timing needs to be appropriate for both yourself and any others involved. There may need to be a period of inaction, waiting till things become clearer and for the right opportunities to present themselves.

Privacy: Keep your journal in a safe place where it cannot be accessed easily by others. You may have an agreement with others close to you concerning confidentiality. Another way to ensure privacy is to use codes for any actions, feelings or people's names that appear regularly. The use of single words rather than sentences also helps.

For further reading
Anne Broyles, *Journalling: A Spirit Journey*, Upper Room, 1994
Edward England, *Keeping a Spiritual Journal*, Highland Books, 1988
Richard Peace, *Spiritual Journalling*, NavPress, 1995
Elizabeth O'Connor, *Letters to the Scattered Pilgrims*, Harper and Row Publishers Inc, San Francisco, 1979
Morton Kelsey, *Adventure Inward*, Alfred A Knopf, New York, 1980
Ira Progoff, *At a Journal Workshop*, Dialogue House, New York, 1975

Some journals to read
Jim Elliott, *The Journals of Jim Elliot*, edited by Elizabeth Elliott, Revell, 1978
Dag Hammarskjöld, *Markings*, translated by W H Auden and Leif Sjoberg, Faber and Faber, 1964
Henri Nouwen, *The Genesee Diary: Report from a Trappist Monastery*, Doubleday, 1976
Helmut Thielicke, *African Diary: My Search for Understanding*, Word, 1974
John Wesley, *The Journals of John Wesley: A Selection*, edited by Elizabeth Jay, Oxford University Press, 1967

STUDY GUIDE

PERSONAL REFLECTION
Try keeping a journal for at least seven days, using the hints given here.
At the conclusion, reflect on the experience using these questions:
• What did you find easy/difficult?
• What feelings surfaced as your journalled?
• What would you do the same or differently in future?
• What became clearer for you?
• What did you learn about journalling?

> **GROUP WORK**
> 1. Share your experiences in journalling.
>   • What did the group learn about journalling?
> 2. Discuss suggestions in this section about the ways journalling can enhance mentoring.

———✳✳✳———

SETTING BOUNDARIES

Not only in mentoring but in every area of our life we need to know what is our task and what isn't, when to say 'yes' and when to say 'no'. This applies particularly to people who care deeply for others. They can assume functions that in the end are not helpful, for they prevent another accepting ownership, taking responsibility for themselves. The issue is one of boundaries. Boundaries help us take control of our lives.

Christians often find this confusing. Christ's law of love, 'love one another', is the distinguishing mark of authentic followers. He said, 'By this will all know you are my disciples' (John 13:34,35). Paul's great passion for Christ and those he served evidenced itself in a reckless commitment: 'Though I am free with respect to all, I have made myself a slave to all, so that I might win more of them. . . To the weak I become weak, so that I might win the weak. I have become all things to all people, that I might by all means save some.' Paul modelled a costly discipleship that is not common today. However, he also strongly emphasised the need for people to take personal responsibility for themselves spiritually: 'This righteousness from God comes through faith in Jesus Christ to all who believe' (Rom 3:22). In Ephesians chapter 4 he says, '. . . live a life worthy of your calling' (v 1); '. . . do not . . .' and 'be . . .' occur a few times. And in chapter 5 he continues encouraging his readers to take responsibility for their own lives, 'Be imitators of God . . .' (v 1) 'live a life of love . . .' (v 2). 'Live as children of light' . . . (v 8).

But lest he be accused of a 'try harder' theology, we must note he emphasises the role of the Holy Spirit in partnership with the believer (Eph 1:13,14,17; 2:18,22; 3:16,20; 4:3,4,30; 5:18; 6:17,18). In his letter to Philippi, there is the same balance, '. . . continue to work out your own salvation with fear and trembling for it is God who works in you . . .' (2:12,13).

Paul puts it well when he says, 'Bear one another's burdens' (Gal 6:2) and then goes on to say, 'all should carry their own loads' (Gal 6:5). The Greek word for 'burden' refers to those things that are beyond our normal ability to carry, while 'load' refers to what is manageable. So this passage is really saying, 'Help those who are struggling with things that they genuinely can't cope with on their own (and be open to receive help yourself when something is beyond you), but let them take responsibility for themselves whenever it is possible for them to do so'.

CONSULT AND BE ACCOUNTABLE

Most people need the support and advice of others in setting and maintaining boundaries. Indeed, boundaries that work are usually best created and kept within a supportive relationship with a friend or mentor. A dramatic illustration of this is Moses. The incredible demands placed upon him from dawn until dusk captured the attention of his father-in-law, Jethro. He helped Moses to set boundaries on this essential work and saved him from burnout (Exod 18).

Where churches or Christian organisations introduce a mentoring system involving a number of mentors, it is advisable to implement a supervisory and support system. Generally this is one skilled person or a small group, who oversees the program. Mentors are guided in establishing appropriate boundaries, kept accountable and are thereby able to seek help for other aspects of their mentoring.

Those who undertake this oversight should be familiar with their church's code of ethics relating to pastoral relationships of ordained and/or lay people. This information may be published as 'Policies Dealing with Complaints of Sexual Misconduct'. Most mainline denominations and some para-church organisations now have these guidelines and provide training in this area.

DISCUSS THE BOUNDARIES

It will be expedient to discuss these with your mentoring partner, together with additional boundaries you each believe should guide your relationship. Discussing all the following may not be appropriate in the first meeting. However, those relating to timing, availability, confidences and respect for boundaries should be addressed early.

117

BE AVAILABLE – WITHIN REASON

Availability is an essential requirement of a good mentor. Some are genuinely too busy with other important things to undertake mentoring effectively. But if people are able to make time available to meet with at least one mentoree they will need to schedule regular time commitments to prevent frustrating their mentoree. Sometimes agreed appointment times will need to be changed, but they can be renegotiated once planned in advance.

Mentors need to be accessible if special legitimate needs arise between planned meetings. I say to all whom I mentor, 'Never hesitate to contact me if you need to'. Some Christian carers, under the guise of being 'professional' erect too many boundaries and limit their availability to set times. Pastors know all too well how often pastoral needs occur outside the hours of '9 to 5'! Some of my most productive mentoring has been done when meeting these emergencies.

KEEP CONFIDENCES

When levels of trust deepen in a mentoring relationship, mentorees feel free to be open and honest about matters they may have not shared with others. They need to be confident they can trust you with anything they tell you. Never, ever, share any confidence without getting their permission, even if it is to seek the prayer support of intercessors. People who can't keep confidences should not mentor.

AVOID EXCESSIVE INTIMACY

While this raises the issue of cross-gender mentoring, same-gender mentoring also presents the need for boundaries. Intimacy, a degree of vulnerability and occasionally potentially arousing subject matter are characteristics of mentoring.

Because of the depth of relationships that can develop, there needs to be clear, understandable, agreed boundaries regarding physical and emotional intimacy, otherwise experience shows there can be disastrous consequences. There are ethical standards that need to guide all caring relationships. Most secular caring professions have ethical guidelines. In the Christian church we have assumed these, although as mentioned earlier, many churches, if they have not spelt them out previously, are now seeing the need to have a clear code of ethics to guide pastoral relationships and ensure that all who work in this area understand them. I strongly advise you to familarise yourself with these guidelines and operate within them.

Mentoring involves deepening levels of trust, and betrayal of that trust through inappropriate behaviour is a serious offence.

The norm in mentoring seems to be women mentoring women and men mentoring men. However, each gender has much to teach and enrich the other through bringing different perspectives to the interaction.

Some people can be quite naive regarding the need for relational boundaries. I mentor younger women leaders. My earlier training in counselling and pastoral care, at theological college under Winston O'Reilly, guides the way I relate to my mentorees. I never mentor in a situation in which I cannot be disturbed – never in my home or theirs, if someone else is not in the house. We generally meet in public areas, such as coffee shops. I am a warm, friendly person who enjoys physical contact. However, without appearing aloof or distant, I have set for myself clear boundaries when helping people. My empathy is conveyed by my body language, attentiveness, my ability to cry, laugh and be silent, my active listening skills and the indwelling Spirit of God. I use touch very sparingly.

It is wise to remember that the purpose of touch is to provide another dimension of support for the person being cared for. It is not to meet the needs of the carer.

Touches can be good, bad or confusing. **Good touches** are touches that make the receiver feel affirmed. **Bad touches** are touches that hurt the receiver. They are experienced by the receiver as manipulative, coercive, abusive or frightening. **Confusing touches** are touches that make the receiver feel uncomfortable, uneasy, confused, unsure. Whether a touch is 'good', 'bad' or 'confusing' is determined by how the receiver experiences it – not by the intentions of the person doing the touching. The 'toucher' may intend the touch to convey a certain kind of message (support, affection, etc), but the message is entirely dependent upon how the receiver perceives the touch and the toucher has no control over this.

Foremost in how the receiver experiences a touch is the element of choice: Does the receiver have a choice in the matter of whether or not to be touched? Is the touch offered, or forced upon the receiver, perhaps on the assumption that the receiver wants to be touched? Is the receiver free to accept or decline the offer? Touch that is not freely chosen by the receiver is likely to be experienced as 'bad' or 'confusing' touch.[7]

ALLOW OTHERS THEIR FREEDOM TO DEVELOP GOD'S WAY

Don't try to force mentorees into your own mould. Don't pressure them to conform to your ideas, your lifestyle or your style of ministry. Help them allow God to get their attention and to respond in faith in order that the Holy Spirit can guide and develop their lives and ministries. Give them the freedom to become the people God intends them to be. The Holy Spirit leads each of us in different paths, often full of great surprises, in sanctifying us and equipping and empowering us for ministry. Christian lifestyle and ministry, while centred firmly in Christ, is tremendously diverse. There are many forms of spirituality, many different gifts of the Spirit, many ways of serving. Don't fall into the trap the Galatians found themselves in and make straightjackets for those you disciple. 'It is for freedom that Christ has set us free . . . called to be free . . . live by the Spirit . . . keep in step with the Spirit' (Gal 3:28; 5:1,12,25).

DON'T BE A PERPETUAL RESCUER

There will be times when we step in to save our mentorees from situations that are beyond them, but such times will be rare exceptions. Repeated rescuing only reinforces irresponsible behaviour. Mentors help their mentorees take responsibility for their lives. There are consequences to all our actions – good or bad, helpful or unhelpful, joyful or sorrowful. What we sow, we reap (Gal 6:7,8). There can be significant learning through reflection on our failures (and our successes). As I emphasise frequently, mentors need to help their mentorees reflect on their experiences to develop self-understanding and insights. This process of reflection is a most important way of averting the dependency factor and leads to the beginning of owning behaviour and emotions and setting the goals for work towards modifying and managing personal issues.

KNOW YOUR OWN LIMITATIONS – ACT AS A BRIDGE TO SPECIALISED RESOURCES

There are times when we are not able to adequately help our mentorees. There are limits to our knowledge and understanding, experience, skills and resources. It is important to be aware of our limits, otherwise our advice and guidance may not be helpful, but even harmful. We never lose face when we admit our limitations, indeed it serves to build confidence. This is the time to act as a bridge to those with more than we ourselves have to offer in certain areas.

However, first consider the frequency and intensity of the problems your mentoree faces. If you suspect outside help is needed, gently raise the issue. Ask if they think it would be beneficial. Most will be relieved that help is available.

I have a list of highly qualified Christian psychologists, a psychiatrist, marriage counsellors, financial consultants, business people, technicians and those with special gifts and skills in ministry to whom I can refer people when necessary. If I don't know the right person to meet the need, I seek guidance from others. It is useful also to know of books and other resources to recommend. If you are not aware of these specialist resources, seek advice from a professionally trained carer. This is one of the advantages of being in a mentoring network with a supervisor, as outlined in Chapter 6, p 150.

ENGENDER RESPECT FOR YOUR BOUNDARIES

Some will want more from us in terms of time, energy, resources and love than we are able to give. Mentorees have been known to become very demanding, even aggressive, manipulative and controlling. We may not be able to set their limits for them, but we can clearly make our own boundaries known and require them to be respected.

Learn to take time out when you need to gain control. Gain confidence in knowing when to say 'yes' and when to say 'no'.

LIMIT THE TIME-SPAN OF YOUR RELATIONSHIP

Some most effective mentoring has lasted for only six or eight sessions – others have continued over years, usually with decreased regularity.

As mentioned elsewhere, it is wise at the commencement to suggest you meet for a short period of, say, three to six meetings, then check how each of you feels and decide whether to continue.

If the relationship continues, from time to time evaluate the process and mentoring effectiveness. This will help ensure the relationship is meeting the needs of the mentoree and is not burdensome for the mentor. It can be simply done by asking, 'How do you think we are going?' . . . 'Are you finding our times helpful?' . . . 'Are there ways we could improve them?' As mentor, you need to also contribute your own response here.

LEARN TO LET GO

While, as mentioned above, some mentoring continues over an extended period, most mentoring has a cut-off point where both agree the purpose for meeting has been fulfilled.

Strong bonds can be developed and there may be difficulty for either or both to let go. There needs to be an acceptance that endings are a natural part of any relationship.

Once it has been agreed that it's time to let go, it is important not to deny or delay the process. A simple closure strategy needs to be followed. This could include:

- openness about feelings evoked
- an overview of how the mentoree thinks he/she has grown and the mentor's reflection on this growth
- recall of God's faithfulness evidenced through specific answers to prayer, guidance, empowerment and other highlights of the times together
- a brief worship celebration focusing on the above, possibly as part of a Love Feast (a modification of a Communion Service)
- an exchange of simple symbolic gifts and a meal or coffee together.

STUDY GUIDE
PERSONAL REFLECTION
1. What boundaries have you set for your relationships with those you help?
   - In what ways has this been helpful?
   - What do you find difficult in seeking to maintain these boundaries?

2. Are there other boundaries mentioned here which you may need to set?
   - How do you feel about that?
   - What will this entail?
3. Can you recall a person betraying your confidence?
   - How did you feel?
   - What problems did it cause?
   - What did you do to try to ensure it wouldn't re-occur?
4. Can you think of a time when a person helping you kept trying to force you into their mould of thinking or behaviour?
   - How did it make you feel?
   - How did you respond?

GROUP WORK

1. Share as much of your personal reflections as you wish.
2. Why do some people, especially those who deeply care for others, have problems setting boundaries?
3. A strong emphasis is placed upon avoiding excessive intimacy. How do you respond to that?
   - In what ways can we show we genuinely care in a relational sense, without being excessively intimate?
4. In what situations as a mentor or co-mentor could we unwisely keep rescuing?
5. Role play *Allowing freedom, Rescuing* or *Knowing your limitations*
6. Why are some carers not willing to acknowledge their limitations?
   - What problems do they create?
7. What are some situations in which we will need to refer people to those with more specialised knowledge, experience and skills than we possess? (Make a list.)
8. Try to identify resource people who could help you in the following ways:
   - by discussing your boundaries
   - by providing specialised resources when you are out of your depth in mentoring another.

—✳✳✳—

ASKING GOOD QUESTIONS

Questions are enormously important. The art of asking good questions is a major factor in effective mentoring. Some would say questions are our master tool.

Jesus used questions frequently – in his contacts with the religious leaders (John 7:19,23; 8:46), in his healing ministry (John 5:6), his transformation of individuals (John 4:7; 8:10), to answer his accusers (John 18:19-24,34), in teaching and mentoring his disciples (John 6:67; 20:15; Matt 16:13-16) and in his suffering (Matt 27:46).

Spending more time asking good questions, and listening rather than talking, is a good rule to follow. Some say at least two-thirds of most mentoring sessions ought to be spent in this mode. Questions help us get into a listening attitude rather than talking too much.

Asking appropriate mentoring questions gets a person thinking for themselves about their situation rather than being dependent upon advice. Questions build confidence and good feelings in a person as they realise they have an active rather than a passive role in the session. They feel valued and significant as a contributor rather than merely a recipient.

Useful information is gathered and issues clarified by good questions. They also can promote action as options are explored and appropriate decisions made about future directions.

Effective questions are easily understood, encourage reflection and refocusing, require thought, clarify issues and enable awareness and disclosure.

There are different types of questions as shown by the following:

OPEN AND CLOSED QUESTIONS

There are many types of useful questions between the two extremes of open and closed questions.

Open questions cannot logically be answered by 'yes' or 'no' – they encourage an answer of more than one word. These questions have degrees of openness ranging from answers of a single word or phrase ('What day will we meet?') to answers requiring an elaborate answer, ('What steps did you take to implement your church mentoring scheme?').

Closed questions, in requiring a yes or no answer, stifle serious thought and the formation of meaningful interpersonal relationships, but have their place, for example in helping to facilitate good listening by indicating the listener's interest and understanding without dominating.

REFLECTIVE QUESTIONS
Reflective questions play a major role in mentoring. They help the revisiting of previous experiences to identify what was actually happening in them in terms of positive and negative feelings and to re-evaluate the experience. Reflective questions, like the following ones, help turn experience into learning:
- What was the experience?
- What was happening?
- What feelings were involved (your own and others)?
- What feelings do you have now as you recall the experience?
- What can you learn from this experience?
- What would you do the same?
- What would you do differently?

SAMPLE QUESTIONS
Here is a further selection of questions to guide you, with a rough framework to fit mentoring sessions. Most of these questions apply to all three dimensions of mentoring, but you will need to be selective. Learn to write your own questions to suit specific situations as these are only a guide. Read through them before each mentoring session, writing down any that appear appropriate. (Check the additional questions in the Appendix.)

Questions for the first or early sessions
Tell me about yourself. (General background. What motivates you? On a scale of 1–10, how would you rate yourself as a people person? What are your strengths – your gifts? What are your growing edges? Tell me about your best friend.)
Tell me about your spouse and family.
Tell me about your relationship to God. (How it really is, not how it ought to be.)
Tell me about your ministry. (What is your vision? What enthuses you? Where are the challenges? How are you feeling about your ministry?)

How can I help you? (See the questions in Chapter 7, Notes for Mentorees, 'Finding a Mentor', p 175, which will help mentorees identify their needs. These could be dealt with here or completed by the mentoree prior to the next session and form the basis for that time.)

Questions for ongoing sessions
Making the connection
(Seek to discover the person's present area of need, and begin there. Goals for action set at the previous session may need to be put to one side or dealt with later if a pressing concern emerges.)
- How are you? – How are you making out?
- How are you **really**? *(If you detect a problem in the way they respond to the first question.)*
- How are you feeling?
- Do you want to talk about it? *(Don't assume they do.)*

Reporting back
- How did you go with the goals we set last time?
- What can we celebrate?
- What have you been able to accomplish?
- What are you finding difficult? How does that make you feel?
- Why do you think that is so?
- What help do you think you may need?

Development of spiritual life
- How are things with you and God?
- How does that make you feel?
- What experiences of prayer and meditation have you had this week?
- What difficulties or frustrations did you encounter?
- What are you doing to improve your knowledge, skills and personal and spiritual development?

Other aspects of personal life
- How are your friendships going?
- How are you maintaining your friendships?
- Tell me about your other relationships.
- How are things at home? *(With spouse and family, siblings.)*

- Tell me about your family's needs and how you are seeking to meet them.
- In what ways will these things we have talked about affect your family/friendships? How?
- What has brought you joy and hope?
- Tell me about how well you sleep?
- What do you do for recreation?

Reflection on ministry

- How is your ministry going? How do you feel about that?
- How does your spouse or your closest friend feel about your ministry?
- What brings you special joy?
- What is of special concern to you?
- What is your greatest challenge and what are you doing to meet it?
- Where is there opposition and how does that make you feel? How are you dealing with it?
- What are you doing to develop relationships with not-yet Christians in the community?
     Community leaders?
     Leaders of other churches?
- In what ways do you show concern for the poor?

Thinking it through together

- What did you find helpful/unhelpful in . . .? How do you feel about it?
- Why do you think that was so?
- What did your spouse/friend think/feel about that?
- What would you do differently – how?
- What do you think Jesus would do in a similar situation?
- Where does God fit in here?
- What does Scripture have to say on this?
- What do you think you could do about . . .? What are you basing that opinion on?
- What are your options? (*Brainstorm if necessary.*)
- Which option seems the most appropriate?
- How do you think that option will help you? *(Particularly if you feel it may not! See also the action/reflection process questions in 'How Adults Learn', p 104.)*

Making an action plan
(Explore all possible angles to the solutions of any problem – brainstorming could be helpful. Evaluate these and prioritise. Get them to think about those at the top of the list. Pray together during this time to try to discern what the Lord is saying in all this.)
- What kinds of things could you work on between now and when we next meet? *(Limit the number – if too many, help them prioritise. Get them to write them out – you make a copy for yourself.)*
- What do you think might prevent you from doing what you want?
   How can you deal with this?
- What or whom do you think could be of help with this?
- Do you know a person whom you respect and trust and with whom you talk that may help make this happen?
   What else could be of help?

Praying it through
- Whom could you ask to pray for you or with you about what we have discussed?
- What is your greatest personal need for which I could pray? *(Now and later)*
- What can I pray for that's a big challenge to you at present? *(Now and later)*

Appraising the relationship
(At previous meeting, indicate that there will be time for appraisal when next you meet so that reflection can be made beforehand.)
- How are your finding our times together?
      what are you finding most helpful – why?
      what are you finding least helpful – why?
      how do you feel about our times together?
- Are your initial expectations being met?
- Are there ways we could improve these times?
- Do you think we have spent sufficient time together or would you like to continue?

Review questions for coaches[8]
(These could be useful in a review process, eg following a mentoree's involvement in a field-work experience with his/her

coach. The questions should relate to the coach's as well as to the mentoree's performance.)
- What was done well?
  - How was that achieved?
- What could have been done better or differently?
  - How could this have been achieved?
- What mistakes were made?
  - How did you feel about these?
  - How can these be avoided in the future?
- What was the most significant learning from this experience?

Brainstorming is suggested a few times both here and elsewhere in the text. For a clear definition, see the section above, 'How Adults Learn', p 104.
(See additional questions in the Appendix.)

—✳✳✳—

ACTIVE LISTENING
THE IMPORTANCE OF LISTENING

In his popular book, *7 Habits of Highly Effective People*,[9] Stephen Covey lists Habit 5 as, **'Seek to first understand'**. We will never understand unless we listen well.

Sensitive, empathetic, concentrated listening to discover what people are really trying to communicate is essential in a mentoring relationship. Indeed it is one of the most important aspects of good mentoring.

Growth is more likely to take place when we can offer this kind of listening to one another. When someone gives us their undivided attention while we are speaking and through their thoughtful feedback prove they have understood what we have said, we are made to feel significant. We feel we matter to this person and they care about us and they love us.

When we really hear another without passing judgment or trying to take responsibility, without trying to mould them, it relaxes them, builds confidence and trust and enables the release of deep feelings, despair and confusion. It enables a person to re-perceive their world in a new way and to go on.

Most of Christ's parables conclude with 'Anyone who has ears, listen'. Each of the letters to the seven churches in the book of

Revelation ends with: 'Anyone who has an ear, listen to what the Spirit is saying . . .' God's complaint in Psalm 81 is: 'O that my people would listen to me'. In his epistle, James exhorts, 'Let everyone be quick to listen and slow to speak' (Jas 1:19). Christ, in his explanation of the parable of the sower, emphasises that each seed which failed stood for someone who had not listened properly and therefore did not grow.

TRUE LISTENING

When love motivates our listening, there is a commitment to not only grasp what is being communicated but also to discover the person behind the words. Empathy is more than a willingness to stand beside a person, it involves a desire to experience as far as possible the speaker's world from inside – to see and feel things from their perspective.

'Listening in dialogue is listening more to meanings than to words . . . in true listening, we reach behind the words, see through them, to find the person who is being revealed. Listening is a search to find the treasure of the true person as revealed verbally and non-verbally.'[10]

Listening does not only mean the physical process of hearing with the ears; it involves an intellectual and emotional process as well, when one's whole being strives to understand and hear the thoughts, feelings and meanings behind the words being uttered. It requires patience, humility, sensitivity, understanding, acceptance and alertness.

An essential aspect of true listening involves the discipline of silence – silence while the other is talking and silence by both to allow time for thoughtful reflection. As someone has put it: 'This silence of love is not indifference; it is not merely poverty of something to say. It is a positive form of self-communication. Just as silence is needed to hear a watch ticking, so silence is the medium through which heartbeats are heard.'[11]

HOW TO LISTEN ACTIVELY
'User-friendly' environments

To assist in giving full attention to each other, try to **avoid environments with distractions**.

Noise can hinder. I conduct the majority of my mentoring sessions in coffee shops or restaurants. Light music in a room with few occupants can help ensure a good degree of privacy. Avoid situations with loud music. Overcrowded places also make it difficult to hear. Meetings in offices or homes have their own distractions which need to be controlled, eg phone, conversations or other noises in adjoining rooms.

Switch off your mobile phone or pager. Have calls diverted.

Lighting. Avoid lighting from natural or artificial sources which shines directly into either's face.

Seating arrangements can distract. Arrange chairs so you are not directly in front of each other – a slight angle avoids threatening eye contact. Don't sit behind a desk with the other person on a chair at a distance. A survey showed 'clients' were five times more at ease where there was no desk. However, where both sat in similar positions at a coffee table, most were at ease.

Space. People have a need for varying degrees of personal space. This applies to proximity both when we stand together and sit. Allow space between seating – not too close and not at a distance – a little more than a metre is a reasonable amount.

Use appropriate body language

Posture is an indicator of your alertness, your attention. Seek to demonstrate relaxed awareness. Incline your body towards the speaker and keep arms and legs uncrossed.

Make appropriate body movements – give positive signals through good eye contact, nodding your head encouragingly, the expression on your face, the sparkle in your eyes and gestures. Keep alert and relaxed.

Give feedback

Active listening means more than simply concentrating on what the other person is saying. It includes letting the other person know that you have heard what he/she has said. It is often useful to check to see if you have heard what the person really intended to communicate.

Communication is often hindered because some have difficulty in translating their thoughts into the words that express what they really mean or feel. Good caring will require feeding back what is received and asking appropriate questions to draw out and help develop the speaker's thoughts.

Paraphrasing: A basic skill involved in active listening is paraphrasing or putting into your own words what the other person seems to be communicating to you. Paraphrasing is a way of testing your understanding of what the other person meant and is always open to being changed. It may not be in the form of a question, but a question mark is always implied. Paraphrasing does not mean approving or agreeing with what the person says, nor is it seeking to reassure, or to probe, or to argue. It is simply letting the other person know they have been heard.

Perception check: These are responses you can make to ensure you are not making false assumptions. Express your own idea of the other person's statement. You may say: 'Is that what you meant?' 'I feel you are disturbed. Did my last statement bother you?' 'I believe we've agreed to meet at the post office corner at 5.00 pm. Is that correct?'

Behaviour description: This involves reporting the specific acts of another to check on your own interpretation of their behaviour and to give opportunity for confirmation or correction by the other person. 'I saw you closing your eyes for a moment. Are you very tired?' 'I saw you jump. Were you startled?' 'I saw you waver and sit down. Are you feeling ill?'

Summarise: Brief summaries of main themes, feelings expressed over a long period of conversation, assures the speaker that he or she is being heard and understood, and helps clarification and gives an integrated picture.

It lets the other person know you are really interested in what they are saying. It shows you want to know what they mean. If the other person feels you can understand their point of view, they are more likely to want to hear your point of view. Paraphrasing can also be useful to the other person in helping them to clarify their own thoughts or feelings by seeing them more objectively or in a different perspective.

Reflecting feelings: Paraphrasing words tests whether or not the listener has heard what the speaker intended to communicate. In a similar way, reflecting the feelings which the listener perceives has been communicated gives opportunity for the speaker to confirm, deny or clarify. Feelings are expressed directly or in metaphor, eg

'I'm angry', 'I feel accepted', 'I'm confused' are direct expressions of feelings. 'I feel as though I'm being treated as a child', 'I feel like something the dog dragged in' are feelings expressed in metaphor.

Being able to recognise and describe the feeling clearly is important if it is to be reflected properly.

Accept the feelings being expressed: Strong negative statements can make us want to reject the feeling coming through to us, but each person has a right to their feelings. It doesn't mean we condone the feelings if we accept them. Caring for people means that none of the feelings they communicate to us, no matter how ugly and repulsive, will make us stop genuinely loving them.

Describe your own feelings: For example, 'I feel warm about your helping me in this way.' 'I am sad to hear about that.' 'I am very anxious about your trip tomorrow.' 'I am very upset with you.' 'After discussing this together, I feel very hopeful.'

Let the other person lead

Invitations to talk: Use simple, non-threatening questions, to indicate your interest, commitment and readiness to listen, such as, 'How are you?', 'How are things going?', 'How did you get on with . . .?', 'How did . . . work out?', 'You look very tired', 'Do you want to talk about . . .?'

Avoid overtalk: One doesn't have to listen to many conversations to notice how frequently people butt in while someone is still talking. Even when the first speaker continues, the intruder proceeds as though they were non-existent. A polite, 'May I contribute here?' or, 'Excuse me but. . .' could be appropriate when someone is dominating or new information is needed. An irritating form of this hijacking is when another completes a speaker's sentence – more annoying when it was not what was intended.

Restrict story-telling: The Bible affirms strongly the importance of story-telling, of recalling God's action in history and retelling to succeeding generations. Our own life experiences and the lessons we learnt through reflection on them are a valuable resource in caring. But the timing of our telling of them is so important. Often when a person is sharing an experience they interlace their conversation with deep feelings. The speaker needs plenty of time and space to process their experience with those listening. If another person barges into the conversation insensitively with 'That reminds me of. . .' or, 'I once had an experience like that', the important time for treatment of the story can be lost. Then another sensitive listener needs to 'rewind the tape' after the intruder has finished and invite the original speaker to continue by saying, 'Do you want to tell us more about your story? How did you feel about . . .' etc. Yes, tell your story – but at the appropriate moment – if one occurs!

Other skills used in active listening

Use 'I' messages: Communication improves when each speaker is willing to take responsibility for their own ideas and feelings and uses the personal pronoun 'I' when it is appropriate. All too often people say something like this: 'After studying this we should take this seriously', rather than indicating they personally have gained new insights and have been challenged, by saying: 'After studying this I'm convinced I should take this seriously'.

A mentor should model in his/her communication a willingness to share directly what he/she feels or thinks by saying 'I', 'my', 'mine', rather than hiding behind generalities. Using personal pronouns to express personal feelings or thoughts directly can deepen the level of communication, avoid indirect or vague messages and develop relationships through greater openness.

Indicate you are with them, using 'little words' and 'non-words': Although we may often say very little, we are by no means entirely passive. We must master the 'little words' – 'sure', 'I see', 'really', 'tell me more', 'go on' – which will facilitate the conversation, as well as assure them we are listening. Even the little grunts of 'ah', 'um', 'huh' are important responses, showing emotional support. A sensitive listener will instinctively know the right moment to interject a quiet word of encouragement or affirmation.

Infrequent questions: Good questions encourage others to think through situations. This involves asking questions without any evaluative judgmental words. Avoid closed questions which have a 'yes' or 'no' response. Use open questions to encourage serious thought, eg 'Had you thought of . . .?' or 'Have you considered . . .?' or 'What about . . .?' or 'What's on your mind?' Be careful, however, to limit the number of these.

Responsive silence: Allow for periods of silence during the conversation. Avoid the temptation to fill these silences – mostly it will be counter-productive. Silence while the other is talking gives assurance of love and acceptance and a sense of warmth and dignity. It facilitates openness and trust. Silence allows the speaker to gather their thoughts, to regain composure, to reflect and to be aware of your supportive presence. It has equal benefit for the listener. Love is often most real in silence.

STUDY GUIDE

PERSONAL REFLECTION

1. Who are the people who really listen to you?
   - How does that make you feel about yourself and about them?
   - What have your learnt from the way they listen to you?
2. How do you feel when people don't listen to you?
   - What have you learnt from those experiences to improve your own listening?
3. In reading this section, what did you discover are your strengths?
4. What weakness, if any, did you identify on which you need to work?
   - What will that involve?
   - Is there someone who can help you in this?

FIELD WORK

Before your next group meeting, practise a few of the suggestions made in this section, your daily conversations at home, in the workplace, in the community and at church. Each day reflect and make notes on:
   - how your listening skills improved
   - ways in which relationships were deepened through better listening
   - responses from those to whom you listened
   - how you felt
   - aspects of listening on which you need to work

GROUP WORK
1. Share aspects of your personal reflection.
2. Field work
   - your general response to your efforts at listening
   - what you learnt by reflecting on ways people listen to you
3. Discuss the importance of active listening for all helping situations.

ROLE PLAY
In normal conversations our listening can be hampered by:
   - our thinking about what we will say while the other person is talking
   - our repeated attempts to be heard
   - the other person's body language and attitude
   - other matters on our minds
   - distractions in the meeting place (people's conversations, noise, etc)

In this exercise, you will experience being listened to well by your partner and, in turn, by you giving your full attention to your partner.

Guard against this time developing into a normal conversation. The focus is on the **process**, how you both listen to each other, rather than the **content** of what you say.

Follow this process carefully:
Begin with one of you acting as the speaker and the other as the listener.
   - In three or four sentences, the speaker gives their response to: 'The thing I enjoy doing most is . . . because . . .'
   - The listener repeats in his/her own words what he/she thinks was said, beginning with 'What I think I heard you say was. . .' (We don't always get it right!)
   - The speaker then repeats what the listener didn't pick up, beginning with 'I may not have made myself clear, so let me repeat what you didn't pick up' (We don't always make it clear).

Once the speaker is satisfied, the roles are reversed and the above repeated.

At the conclusion of the allocated time, reflect together on this experience.
- Choose a 'feeling word' to describe how you feel after this exercise (eg closer, stimulated, frustrated, warm, inspired, discouraged, loved, despondent, elated, encouraged, motivated to improve these skills, etc)
- What did you enjoy about this exercise?
- What did you find difficult?
- In what ways do you need to improve your ability to listen well?
- How will you do this?

—✳✳✳—

MORE GUIDELINES FOR MENTORS
TAKE THE RESPONSIBILITY SERIOUSLY

As with all aspects of Christian service, mentoring is a **sacred responsibility**. It is another significant aspect of Christ's ongoing ministry through his followers. Mentoring is for those who are able and prepared to give it the time and effort it requires. However, it has its rich rewards as one sees others maturing in Christ and gaining confidence and competency in their service for him. I have had a varied and most fulfilling ministry over more than forty years – mentoring has been one of its highlights.

This chapter began by drawing attention to the crucial **role of prayer** in all our service for Christ. Take seriously the suggestions made there regarding keeping your own relationship with God fresh and vital.

Seek to be accountable to a peer or a more experienced person regarding the way you are handling your mentoring. Don't discuss confidences but talk over difficulties and get them to ask you the hard questions about your own spiritual and personal life and your compassion for and commitment to those you mentor.

Prepare for each mentoring session. Review your notes, scan the list of questions in this chapter and the Appendix, then make a list of items you feel you should raise and questions to ask. (However, be flexible in how you use these notes.) There may also be some resources to hand on to others, which you need to photocopy. Act upon any promises made or issues you need to pursue (see the note here on Follow-up).

DEGREES OF INTENSITY VARY

We need to keep in mind that the degree of intensity varies in mentoring. Sometimes, in working with my mentorees, I find I am helping them with deep personal and spiritual issues while at other times our meetings are very informal. On these latter occasions there is affirmation and encouragement – little more than just being together, sharing good fellowship and celebrating God's faithfulness.

When dealing with peer mentoring, I have pointed out the need to be aware of the variable nature of mentoring, maintaining the balance of not being too hard or too easy with each other.

Some reading this book may feel that they are incapable of mentoring at the depths dealt with in various sections.

Let me emphasise again that mentoring is a very significant role every Christian disciple can fulfil, irrespective of age or experience. We can all enrich another person's life through words of encouragement and a wise word from time to time. The degree to which any one of us can help will vary greatly. In retrospect, however, a seemingly insignificant word, a willingness to listen, or a brief prayer can often be seen to have made an impact upon another far beyond our expectations.

THE FIRST MEETING

I seldom if ever commit myself to mentor another without suggesting we first have a meeting to talk about the possibility. I see this as a **time for assessment**, gauging if there is chemistry between us, if we feel comfortable with each other, if there is a sense of bonding.

This time begins by **getting to know each other** (see 'Design for Mentoring – Assessment Session, p 144, and 'Ask Good Questions', p124 in this chapter, for the first or early sessions).

I then **share** my understanding of the aims and purpose of mentoring. This helps the other person to clarify their own perceptions and consider if this is their expectation. I find having them read a book on mentoring beforehand helps here.

The next phase in this initial meeting is for me to **understand what is expected of me**. So I usually ask 'What are you hoping to get out of our relationship?' . . . 'In what ways do you think I can help you?'

This brings us to be honest about our gut feelings in the light of this brief encounter – to seek to **assess whether we are meant to continue**. If I don't feel the person is serious enough about the commitment involved, I suggest they think further about it and contact me later if they wish. Occasionally I have to say I don't think I have a strong background in the area in which help is being sought and may refer them to others.

If we both feel we should continue then we become quite intentional about the following:

Setting a time frame
- **for frequency of meeting**, usually every four to six weeks. But this can vary greatly. With people living at a distance, eg interstate or overseas, we meet each time I am in their area or use the phone or e-mail.
- **for the initial length of the relationship.** It is better to meet for a shorter than an extended period. I usually suggest six meetings. This allows us to evaluate and decide to continue or to terminate.

Agreeing on some guideposts regarding honesty, accountability, confidentiality, the role of prayer, assignments, the place of the Scriptures and my availability outside of the sessions.

PRACTISE MUTUAL ACCOUNTABILITY
I have introduced above the importance of agreeing on, among other things, accountability. This must never be one-sided. There needs to be an agreed mutual accountability by both mentor and mentoree to the goals and purpose of the mentoring relationship and sessions. I have mentioned mutual accountability for peer mentoring, but it should apply to all mentoring relationships. We should never have expectations of those we lead regarding aspects of accountability that we are not prepared to carry out ourselves.

However, this accountability must be guided by biblical principles. In the section 'Walking the Road Together' p 34, I have sought to briefly provide some understanding of this. Let me reiterate here the spirit in which this is to be administered. God's grace is the governing factor.

Rod Denton, in the section he contributed in Chapter 6, 'Mentoring a Ministry Team in the Local Church' (p 156), illustrates well the need for mentors to see themselves accountable to their mentorees in terms of their integrity and credibility by means of their modelling.

SEEK OUT THEIR REAL NEEDS

The presenting need, what a person initially states is their need, may not be their real need. You may not be a trained counsellor with the skills to discover this but keep alert, ask good questions and you could find yourself being guided by the Spirit to mentor in a different area to that first raised.

SETTING ASSIGNMENTS

We should expect mentorees to be prepared to undertake work between meetings. Mentors will enable their mentorees to set goals and actions during most meetings. Mostly these assignments will grow out of the mentoree's response to the question, 'In the light of all we have talked about, what do you now think you should be doing?' (see the action/reflection process questions in 'How Adults Learn' (see p 104) and questions under 'Asking Good Questions', 'Thinking It Through Together' and 'Making an Action Plan', pp 124ff.) Mentors contribute to this process, making suggestions for their consideration.

Sometimes I am directive, giving them an assignment such as a book, or copy of an article to read, a person to interview, a situation to observe, a case study to consider or a video or audio cassette to view or hear. Occasionally, I suggest a passage of Scripture to study and explore its relevance. Then the report they bring to the next session becomes the basis of much of our time together. When they attend a learning event, we reflect on this at the next meeting.

GOAL SETTING

A few guidelines about goal setting will help. The purpose of goal setting is to encourage being intentional rather that reactive in both life and ministry. Goals should be **clear and understandable** (concrete rather than abstract), **measurable** (there will be a clear indication when it has been achieved), **achievable**, and have a

realistic time frame in which to be achieved. It will help to state the goal briefly but then write in a sentence the **desired outcome** (ie what a specific situation, etc, will be like when the goal is achieved).

A few **steps** to be taken **to achieve the goal** should be listed to give some clear signposts to follow.

BE OPEN AND HONEST

When it is appropriate, tell of your own failures and the lessons you learnt when you spent time reflecting on those experiences. Don't try to appear as a paragon of virtue or one who always succeeds. They will find it easier to identify with you in your honesty and be encouraged as you testify to God's undeserved kindness in forgiving and restoring you.

It will be appropriate occasionally to admit your own needs and seek their support. On the occasions I do this, the bond between us has been strengthened.

BE PREPARED TO BE FIRM

Be gentle, as mentorees may be under stress. Don't lay unnecessary burdens on others. However, there are times when we need to be firm. Jesus said, 'If another disciple sins, you must rebuke the offender . . .' (Luke 17:3). Timothy was instructed by Paul to 'correct, rebuke and encourage' (2 Tim 4:2) and Titus was to 'encourage and rebuke with authority' (Titus 2:15). There are times when we need to reprimand, to sanction, to be willing and able to confront.

One of my mentorees said to me, 'Tell me when you think I'm heading into trouble; help me recognise the dangers ahead, warn me when I'm at risk.'

But remember, encouragement is used frequently in the Scriptures. Timothy and Titus were instructed to encourage. Never leave another discouraged, always combine rebuke with encouragement and hope, based on the overwhelmingly sufficient grace of God in Christ.

KEEP RECORDS/NOTES

I keep notes of my mentoring sessions in a section of my expandable diary/organiser. This means I have it always with me to use during meetings with mentorees and in between times for follow-up and prayer. Others keep a separate log-book for their mentoring – some have one for each mentoree.

I record the following:

- Mentoree's details – name, address, phone and fax numbers, e-mail
- Names of spouse, children (ages)
- Date of each meeting
- Notes taken during the session (sparingly) – relevant points, assignments, follow-up
- Date and place for next meeting
- Date for review

Build in Some Serendipity

Plan some happy surprises! Celebrate major birthdays, wedding anniversaries, etc. Vary the venue of your meetings. Occasionally hike or play golf together. Spend a day or half-day in retreat together.

Take an Interest in Their Spouse and Family

Know their names. Talk unhurriedly to whoever answers the phone. Keep in regular contact when there is a crisis.

Be Willing to Receive

Frequently I'm challenged and inspired by my mentorees' enthusiasm, idealism, vision, dedication, resourcefulness and much, much more! I seek to affirm that and tell how it blesses me. They often introduce me to resources which I find helpful – in being open to receive, my own life and ministry is enriched.

Do Your Follow-up

Write into your daily check list items for follow-up made in your session notes – contacts to make, resources and information to seek out, etc.

Learn to Use Your Phone

Keep contact by phone (or written note) between regular meeting times when you feel the need to, especially if your friend or mentoree is struggling or circumstances hinder regular meetings. I mentor a number who live at a significant distance. Face-to-face contact is very irregular. The phone at off-peak periods is our main contact. Develop confidence to pray on the phone.

CELEBRATE WINS

One mentoree said, 'All my previous mentor did was tell me where I was wrong. He never affirmed or encouraged me.' I enjoy asking, 'What can we celebrate today?' There is usually something for which we can be genuinely thankful in the gloomiest situation – an answer to prayer, signs of hope, experiences of the faithfulness of God and his people and indications of change. Celebrate together evidences of God's grace. Rejoice and praise God with them. Show some excitement. While mentoring in a coffee shop I've sometimes ordered a cake each and an extra cup of coffee to celebrate!

TRUST THEM TO GOD

God, the Holy Spirit is the mentor – we are but the channels of grace. Build their attachment to Christ, not yourself. When we learn to release our friends or mentorees to God and trust them to him, there are often some beautiful surprises – but not always immediately! He can do what we can't.

STUDY GUIDE

PERSONAL REFLECTION

1. What previous experiences may have been improved by you or another person involved, if you had practised some of the suggestions mentioned here?
   • In what ways would it have made a difference?
2. Why is it important to build in some serendipity and celebrate wins?
   • When did someone do this for you?
   • How did you respond?
3. How do you feel when another person is not prepared to receive encouragement or other support from you?
   • How do you think mentorees feel when their mentors are open to receive from them?

> **GROUP WORK**
> 1. Share your individual work.
> 2. What 'wins' by a group member or the group as a whole can you celebrate?
>   • How and when will you do this?

A DESIGN FOR MENTORING SESSIONS

The following is a rough guide. You will need to be sensitive, alert and flexible in order to respond appropriately. (See 'Asking Good Questions', p 124, to fill this out.)

INITIAL INQUIRY
'Would you be willing to be my mentor?'
'Let's meet to talk about it and see how we both feel.'

ASSESSMENT SESSION

Get Acquainted – 'Tell me about yourself' *(Background, present situation, interest, vision and dreams).*

Identify Needs – 'How do you think I can help you?' *(Discuss and clarify)*

(If you feel you are not the appropriate person, explore other possibilities with them.)

(If you both agree you are the right person to help then . . .)

Agree on a time frame – 'How often would you like to meet?'
– 'For what period?' *(Set a date for evaluation)*

Introduce other matters – eg keeping a mentoring journal, etc. (see p 113)

How can I help you now? – 'Do you have any matters you would like to talk over now?' *(Discuss)*

Agree on an assignment – 'What do you think you could be working on for our next meeting?' *(Discuss – make your own copy.)*

Pray together

Ongoing Sessions
Start where they are
'How are you?' *(Watch the body language – if it doesn't match the verbal response, ask . . .)*
'But how are you really?'
'How can I help you today?' *(problems, questions, issues the person wants to deal with.)*
(Needs which surface here may form the basis for much, if not all your time on this occasion.)
Report on assignment
'How did you go with the assignment on which we agreed last time?'
Discussion of ongoing or new areas of need
'On what do you want to continue working, or is there another area we should talk about?' – 'Tell me about it.'
'What scriptural principles need to be taken into account here?'
'What do you think you could do about . . .?'
'Are there any other options?'
Begin to help them build a prayer base
'Whom could you ask to pray for or with you about this?'
Agree on a new assignment
'What do you think you could be working on for our next meeting?'
(Discuss – Make your own copy.)
Pray together

STUDY GUIDE
GROUP WORK
Role Play
Do role plays of both an assessment and an ongoing session. Discuss each as a group.

[1] Eugene H Peterson, *Foreword to New Testament Spirituality* by Michael Green and R Paul Stevens, Eagle, 1994
[2] *Seize the Day with Dietrich Bonhoeffer*, Charles Ringma, Albatross Books, 1991, 9 July
[3] Ed, Walter A Elwell, Baker, Bookhouse, Grand Rapids, 1991
[4] Oxford, 1997

[5] *A Spiritual Formation Journal*, Jana Rea with Richard J Foster, Harper, San Francisco, 1992

[6] Rea with Foster

[7] Based on the Touch Continuum as presented by Cordelia Anderson in *The Child Sexual Abuse Prevention Guidebook*, © 1992; Sexual Assault Services, Hennepin County Attorney's Office, Minneapolis MN, 1979

[8] See '99 Excellent Coaching Questions' (pages 2:13 to 2:16) in *Empowering Leaders Through Coaching* by Steven L Ogne and Thomas P Nebel, Direction Ministry Resources, City, 1995

[9] *The 7 Habits of Highly Effective People*, Stephen R Covey, Simon and Schuster, 1989

[10] *Why am I afraid to tell you who I am?* John Powell

[11] Source unknown

CHAPTER 6

STRATEGIES FOR MENTORING

MENTORING NEW CHRISTIANS

Growing to become the person God wants us to be is a long-term goal, requiring all the help available through the Holy Spirit working directly with us and through other Christians.

Paul knew the importance of caring for new Christians and helping them mature.

'For you know that we dealt with each of you as a father deals with his own children, encouraging, comforting and urging you to live lives worthy of God, who calls you into his kingdom and glory' (1 Thess 2:11,12, NIV).

'So be on your guard! Remember that for three years I never stopped warning each of you night and day with tears' (Acts 20:31, NIV).

Christian fellowships which take seriously their care of new Christians assign sensitive, mature persons to take a special interest in and mentor new disciples. They do this by making them feel wanted, helping them through their doubts and fears, personally introducing them to other encouraging believers and by praying for them and discipling them.

In addition to this one-to-one care, new Christians should be linked to a nurture group as soon as possible after they have decided to follow Christ. Nurture groups are short-term groups, usually lasting six to eight weeks, which provide support to help new disciples of Christ begin their life together in a caring fellowship of Christian love. The group consists of some experienced Christians as well as the beginners. A nurture group is a bridge into the wider fellowship of a local church.

Here are a few things I have found helpful in fostering beginners in the way of Christ. I list them here in summary form, as there is an abundance of resources available in Christian bookshops that develop these themes.

In mentoring new Christians one-to-one and in small groups, I have covered most of these briefly in the initial meetings and then dealt with them at a greater depth later.

- **Help them integrate into a warm, welcoming fellowship** (Luke 15:3-7). Accompany them. Introduce them to other loving believers. Sit with them.
- **Take them through the steps of faith in Christ** to ensure they have made a clear commitment to Christ. (Rom 5:8; Rom 3:22,23; Eph 2:8,9; John 1:12; 2 Cor 5:17)
- **Develop their sense of assurance** – teach them how they can be sure they are right with God through:
  The outer witness – evidences of change in attitude and behaviour. (John 1:12,13; 20:31)
  The inner witness – the Holy Spirit giving inner certainty. (Rom 8:16; 1 John 3:24; 4:13; 5:10
  The witness of Scripture – Certainty grows as we understand and believe what God promises (1 John 5:13; John 1:12,13; 20:31)
- **Explain the '1, 2 and 3' of the Christian life:**
1. All are **one** in Jesus Christ – we need each other. (Eph 4:25)
2. Christians have **two** natures – (Gal 5:16-25; 2 Cor 5:17; Col 3:5-17) Paul describes them as 'flesh' (self-centredness, living as though there were no God) and 'spirit' (God-centredness, seeking to live a life empowered by God's Spirit to please and honour him). The Christian life is essentially a **partnership** of two, not a solo performance. A disciple of Christ is one plus the Holy Spirit. (Rom 8:22,26; John 14:16,26)
3. There are **three** parts to salvation,
   - **past** – freedom from **penalty** of sin (1 John 1:9)
   - **present** – freedom from **power** of sin (Rom 6:5-11)
   - **future** – freedom from **presence** of sin (Rom 5:9,10; 1 Cor 15:55-57)
- **Show that conversion is just a beginning.** We need to grow (Eph 4:15) – teach them how to grow. This involves **deepening**

and maintaining our relationship with God (Eph 4:15; Phil 3:8-19). Growth takes place as we use the channels of God's life-transforming grace (prayer, Bible, fellowship, obedience, worship, sacraments). Be sure to focus on the 'how', not merely the 'ought'.

- **Enable them to understand that the Holy Spirit is the key to godly living.** Explore what the Bible teaches, and encourage them to claim by faith all the resources of the Spirit that are readily available to them. (John 16:15; Eph 5:16-26; 1 Cor 12:1-11)

- **Encourage them to apply the Scriptures to their lives** (James 1:22-25) by asking themselves, 'How is God trying to get my attention here?', 'In what ways would I be different if I took this seriously?' and 'Whom will I ask to pray for me as I seek to put this into practice?'

- **Teach them that they will experience opposition, but God gives us grace to meet it.** Ephesians is a good book to study in this regard. Paul faces the reality of our struggles (6:12), presents a big picture of God and the riches of our relationship with him in Christ (1:3-10, 18-23; 2:4-10, 13-22; 3:14-21), the powerful role of the Holy Spirit (1:17; 2:18; 3:16; 5:18; 6:17,18) and our equipment to live successfully (6:10-18).

- **Help them understand how to deal with temptation and failure.** (1 Cor 10:12,13; Matt 26:41; Heb 4:15; 1 John 1:9)

- **Motivate them to serve.** Help them to serve according to their natural abilities, acquired skills and their spiritual gifts. Assistance will be needed in discovering, developing and using their spiritual gifts (Rom 12:6-8; 1 Cor 7:7; 1 Cor 12:4-11). Their homes, workplaces, the community as well as the church will all be presented as places where they are to serve.

- **Encourage them to share their faith** to in order to grow themselves and bring others to faith in Christ (Acts 1:8). Be sure to give them help in learning how to do this, guided and empowered by the Holy Spirit.

- **Don't give them too much too soon.**

- **Spend time with them doing things they enjoy doing,** to get to know them and build your relationship.

STUDY GUIDE

PERSONAL REFLECTION

1. What assistance did you receive as a new Christian?
   - How did it help?
   - How did it make you feel?
2. If you didn't receive any, what would you have appreciated?
3. Which of the items listed here has been especially meaningful to you personally? In what way has it helped?

GROUP WORK

1. What can we learn from Paul in this aspect of mentoring? *(Refer to the Scripture passages at the commencement.)*
2. Share your individual work.
3. What books and/or other resources relating to the various areas for development listed here have you found useful?

—✳✳✳—

MENTORING AND SMALL GROUPS

Mentoring can play a major role in enabling individual groups and networks of groups to be more effective.

MENTORING LEADERS OF SMALL GROUPS

Some of the best small-group networks I have observed have in place a mentoring strategy to support and develop each small-group leader. In a small network with only a few groups this may be done by the most experienced of their leaders. Sometimes this will be the pastor, or more frequently, the person responsible for coordinating the groups. This is done one-to-one and when the cluster of leaders all meet together with their common mentor. The frequency of these meetings varies. Even an occasional meeting with the mentor can be very supportive. However, John Allison, who heads up the large network of small groups at Redcliffe Uniting Church in Brisbane, provides each leader with one-to-one encouraging support every two weeks and with a group of other leaders monthly.

In the **one-to-one meetings** the focus is upon issues related to leadership of the group – leadership style, keeping the group life vital, understanding and helping group members, helping members to learn and keep growing, etc. However, the leader's personal, family and spiritual life will also be covered. Prayer relating to the matters discussed will be an important element.

When the **leaders' support group** meets, the focus is upon the ongoing development of group and leadership skills. The mentor will enable the leaders to be open to God and each other so that this same openness will reproduce itself in the groups represented. Time will be given to discuss difficulties encountered, to celebrate successes, to share ideas, resources and new insights gained while leading their groups, to care for one another and to worship and pray together. To effectively fulfil these roles, this group meets every four to six weeks. At Redcliffe church, mentioned above, their strong emphasis upon leadership support provides this experience every two weeks for new leaders, moving to four-weekly once they become more competent.

This is sometimes extended by ongoing, more **informal mentoring** among the leaders themselves as they meet in pairs to co-mentor each other in between leaders' gatherings.

In **large networks** where a tree-like support structure is used, the leaders are grouped in fives under the oversight of a more experienced person at each level. What is outlined above then operates in this framework, both one-to-one and in leaders' clusters.

MENTORING EMERGING SMALL-GROUP LEADERS

Jesus identified three emerging leaders in his group – Peter, James and John. He exposed them to some intimate moments in his life – the raising of Jairus' daughter, his transfiguration on the mountain and in the second stage in the Garden of Gethsemane. All three became the leaders of the early church. But Peter seemed to receive special mentoring, and he undoubtedly became the most influential leader of the three.

One of the best seedbeds for identifying and beginning to develop new leadership of small groups is a healthy, growing group. More often, new leaders emerge from one-to-one mentoring when someone is keen to learn and serve Christ. An effective leader will provide a good model and give opportunities to identify, affirm, develop and use the new potential leader's gifts, providing needed support and ongoing mentoring.

Group leaders need to know **how to recognise** members of their group with leadership potential and **how to nurture** them. This is a most demanding and difficult skill for leaders to acquire. There is undoubtedly a spiritual giftedness dimension to this ability to raise up new leaders. However, confidence will be gained through modelling by those possessing this ability and some training in how to recognise group members with the potential for leadership. It will be emphasised that a potential leader needs to **learn to serve** before a leadership position or role is offered.

Leaders should **consult** with their own personal mentors and leaders' group to confirm their own convictions regarding a possible new leader. When endorsed, the person can be invited to participate in most activities for leaders.

The emerging leader will be given **increasing responsibilities** with the group leader more intentionally providing mentoring, support and encouragement and evaluating performance together. The group, of which the emerging leader is a member, will be kept informed of these developments and they, along with the wider community, will be given opportunity to **affirm and endorse** the apprentice leader.

MENTORING IN DISCIPLESHIP GROUPS

The different types of groups that have as their specific purpose the making of disciples, provide a further opportunity for mentoring. The group should be kept small enough to permit the leader to mentor each member outside of the group's gathered life. Even if this occurs infrequently when a member needs special care, it will enhance both the lives of the individual and the group as a whole.

Encouraging members to enter into co-mentoring relationships with each other will provide personal and spiritual support between meetings. Issues dealt with in the group can be processed further and another dimension of aid and accountability experienced.

MENTORING IN SPIRITUAL FORMATION GROUPS

In-depth spiritual formation groups and accountability groups come in various forms.

Groups of three or four people meeting with the express purpose of taking their discipleship more seriously virtually fulfil a peer mentoring function. Many of these groups follow none of the better-known formats but **make a simple covenant to 'watch over one another in love'**. They seek to understand the teachings of Jesus, apply them to each aspect of their lives, be open with God and each other, be accountable and faithfully and graciously support each other.

One of the most effective spiritual formation group movements is that spawned by Richard Foster's writings. Here all levels of mentoring are often found operating – group mentoring, co-mentoring and mentor/mentoree relationships.

Richard Foster's best-selling book *Celebration of Discipline* encouraged many to seek a deeper spirituality. However, frustration was experienced by many because of lack of intentionality and balance.

Foster teamed with James Bryan Smith to develop what has proved to be a most effective small-group model similar to that used by John Wesley in eighteenth-century England.

These spiritual formation groups, which are proving so effective in nurturing a balanced spirituality, have become known as **Renovaré groups** (from the Latin, meaning 'to renew'). They are based on the five spiritual dimensions that we see in the early church and later movements: contemplative *(the prayer-filled life)*; holiness *(the virtuous life)*; charismatic *(the Spirit-empowered life)*; social justice *(the compassionate life)*; evangelical *(the word-centred life)*.

When all five of these traditions are active in a group, they bring balance and wholeness to the Christian life and mission.

These form the basis of the Renovaré group covenant. Mutual accountability helps maximise this group agreement, facilitating balance and wholeness under the guidance and empowerment of the Holy Spirit.

The manual for Renovaré groups is *A Spiritual Formation Group Workbook* and the major resource is the *Devotional Classics*. Both are by Richard Foster and James Bryan Smith and were published by Harper, San Francisco, in 1993.

In the Appendix you will find the Renovaré Self-examination Questions.

LIFE TRANSFORMATION GROUPS[1]

Peer mentoring and discipling of pre-Christian friends is the focus of Life Transformation Groups being introduced into numerous churches. An LTG is made up of two to three people, all of the same gender, who meet weekly for personal accountability for their spiritual growth and prayer for one another and others.

There are two main elements of accountability. One element is open, honest sharing based on the Ten Questions of Accountability *(listed in the Appendix)*. The other is reporting on how God has gained each person's attention through the individual, regular reading of large passages of Scripture. As well, each member identifies two not-yet Christian people, who become a prayer focus for the whole group. A specific prayer guide directs these prayers.

When groups grow past three, they divide into two groups.

Danny Greenwood, Director of Small Groups at Mount Evelyn Christian Fellowship in Melbourne, Victoria, has found that the strength of the LTGs lies in their simplicity. In time, any participant will be able to start a group of their own. Beginning an LTG is as simple as finding one other willing participant and then eventually recruiting one other person each. The shortest time he has been in a group before dividing was three months, the longest being three years.

John Allison, mentioned earlier, has introduced an adaptation of these small cells into his church. He comments:

'In the average small group, many of the group members can tend to sit back and drift with the flow of the group. Many do not necessarily experience life-changing growth or become competent at "making disciples".

'These groups do not need "leaders". We have established a balanced group process that a person of any experience can follow. As participants share with one another the joys, successes and frustrations of their own faith and life journey, and the impact of the Scripture on their day-to-day life, peer mentoring takes place as a natural consequence.

'So far, five different sets of accountability questions/life issues have been developed covering application to: (i) senior ages, (ii) young adults, (iii) new Christians/seekers, (iv) family age men and (v) family age women.'

STUDY GUIDE

INDIVIDUAL REFLECTION

1. 'Watching over one another in love'.
   - 'Watching over' has a negative image for many because of past experiences. What aspects of this have you experienced, and how did that make you feel?

     How have you seen this being avoided in small groups?
   - In what ways have you experienced being cared for 'in love'?

     What did that mean to you personally?

     What did you learn about caring?
2. Try to summarise in a few sentences what you learnt here about the role mentoring can play in a small group.
3. Jesus was concerned about people as whole beings – both soul and body. He healed people physically, mentally, emotionally and spiritually. He showed concern for the hungry and the disadvantaged. He acted in anger towards injustice.
   - What concerns you deeply about these areas of need? (Think of specific people and situations.) What feelings surface when this comes to mind?

     What could you individually, or with some others, do to show your concern?
   - In what ways can we keep this balance in our mentoring and co-mentoring?
   - How would you adapt the Renovaré questions on Social Justice/The Compassionate Life (see *Appendix*) for use in an LTG group?

IN SMALL GROUPS

1. Discuss your individual work.
2. Why is it important to provide mentoring for small-group leaders?
3. Share your adaptation of the Renovaré questions.
4. The Transforming Life Cells developed at Redcliffe have five sets of different accountability questions.
   - How would you modify the Life Transformation Group's questions (found in the Appendix) to suit your age and interest group?
   - What further questions would you find helpful?

—✳✳✳—

MENTORING A MINISTRY TEAM

A TEAM IN THE LOCAL CHURCH

Rod Denton has led ministry teams in Melbourne for nine years, in his role as Youth Pastor at Blackburn Baptist Church (now Crossway), and as Senior Pastor of Clovercrest Baptist Church in Adelaide for five years. In both situations he has placed a high priority on raising up church staff from within the membership of the church and then creating a mentoring environment within the growing ministry team.

At the time of writing, the ministry team of his church has a membership of eight and the voluntary leadership community has grown to over one hundred.

The following are some key characteristics of the mentoring environment that Rod Denton actively seeks to develop within the senior ministry teams that he leads:

Ministry team (peer) mentoring

A foundational key to team mentoring is to create a team spirit in which members of the team are able to interact with one another in such a way that they will have a significant input into one another's lives. This is achieved by building regular meeting times into the team's agenda, where team members come together to:

- share a meal in an informal atmosphere (usually Sunday lunch each month, with families),
- meet to review and plan their ministries, reflect together on study books and articles, and pray for one another (usually Monday morning each week), and
- take occasional retreats away.

The goal of these activities is to build a supportive team spirit whereby members can encourage and learn from one another from their collective wisdom and ministry experiences.

Attitudinal mentoring

The attitude of the team leader is a critical component in the empowerment of team members. Consequently I always seek (but have not always succeeded!) to:

- believe in my team members and encourage them to believe in themselves,

- to continually see each member through the eyes of Jesus and be potential oriented, and
- to expect that each team member grow to a level of proficiency beyond mine in their focused area of ministry.

Formal mentoring

My goal as a team leader has been to establish a regular meeting time with each member (either weekly or fortnightly). There I focus on his/her weekly report sheet, covering goal setting and progress achieved, ministry review, skills development, study and reflection of relevant books, cassettes and articles, personal and family matters, and prayer. This meeting usually lasts about an hour, and occurs in my office, in a nearby restaurant or while walking together around the local neighbourhood.

Resource mentoring

Because I cannot personally be responsible for all aspects of a team member's mentoring, I work with each member to see how their personal growth and ministry development can be enhanced by ensuring that they be exposed to key resources that become available from time to time. Consequently, I need to keep continuously abreast of the range of training and learning opportunities that are being released and maintain a budget for such opportunities. The provision of resources for team members can include books, cassettes, videos, seminars (both local and interstate) and networking opportunities that become available with resourceful leaders. As a team leader, I believe I need to continually be investing in team members in this way so that they are being exposed to the best available resources in order that their personal and ministry development can be maximised.

Sponsorship mentoring

It is my goal to continually provide open doors for ministry team members where they will have growing opportunities to minister within and beyond the local church to expand their level of influence and gain valuable experience that will hasten their own growth curve. Sponsorship mentoring is also achieved by opening doors for team members by linking them with key leaders in their own area of giftedness and occasionally delegating to them ministry invitations that come to me.

Personal mentoring

As team leader, my accountability is primarily to the church council elected by the church members. However, I see myself also accountable to the team I lead, especially in terms of my personal integrity and the integrity of my ministry.

I will never forget one of my team members saying to me, 'Rod, be careful how you live your life, because I am observing you and following your example.' Paul said, 'Therefore, I urge you to imitate me' (1 Cor 4:16). It's a great responsibility to realise that a leader will usually reproduce after his/her own kind. And not only the leader, for my wife, Sue, was deeply touched the day one of my team members wrote her a note to say he was looking for a wife that displayed the caring qualities that she had lived out in his presence in our home. With this aspect of mentoring in mind, it is of interest to note that Sue has found unusual delight in noticing some of my team members displaying some of my unique idiosyncrasies in the course of their public ministry.

Reciprocal mentoring

One of the great encouragements of adopting such a strategy as this is that I, as the team leader, personally benefit from this process. I am immeasurably enriched by their input into my life and their care for me and my family. As a result, deep friendships are formed with team members. These continue beyond our ministry time together and I find that our friendship overflows into my social and family life.

In summary, team mentoring is:
- critical for the health and growth of the church and its staff
- based on relationships of trust, humility and mutual care
- undergirded by continuous prayer
- costly in time, personal finances and the sacrifice of personal achievements
- seen as a threat to Satan's purposes in a church, and becomes a target for spiritual warfare
- only made possible with people who desire to serve as team members, where they willingly accept responsibility for the growth of other team members and are supportive of the team leader, in spite of his/her patent shortcomings

- based on the model of ministry developed by Jesus with his disciples, then
- modelled by each team member as they relate to their own ministry team in the department in which they serve.

A TEAM OF VOLUNTEERS

Kate Helm has been a Scripture Union volunteer since high school student days in Victoria. Her experience has been on camps for secondary age teens, SU Family Missions on the beach and in inner-city settings. As recent co-founder and director of the Carlton Estate SU Family Mission, she describes much of her responsibility for such a team in the spirit of 2 Timothy 2:2 – 'You have heard me teach. Now I want you to tell these same things to followers who can be trusted to tell others.'

'I was mentored faithfully and intentionally by others, although I wasn't actually aware of it at the time. This mentoring arose out of the belief that God creates each person as a unique individual with a specific purpose for his/her life; it is not the result of some sort of program designed to "process" Christians. As a member of a team of volunteers I was related to as a person with God-given capacities, gifts, personality and experience; **I was not just one of a group working to accomplish a common goal**. My mentors were aware that I needed personalised guidance, support and plenty of encouragement. I was allocated tasks that suited my giftednesss and maturity – tasks that would stretch me and enable me to develop as a leader. They recognised my potential, believed in me and took risks with me. They had more confidence in me than I had in myself.

'Now I lead a team of volunteers who conduct a short-term community-based holiday program. Much effort is involved in developing and maintaining a team of diverse individuals. To achieve our specific task is a balancing act! We have a leadership group which we call a cooperative, where our thinking and planning occurs. Different areas of responsibility are shared among this leadership group according to their gifts and experience. Together we set the direction and priorities of the program but we do not prescribe how various aspects are to be carried out. All involved, whether up-front or behind-the-scenes are enabled to minister in a way that matches God's unique equipping of each individual. Personal initiative and responsibility are therefore developed in an atmosphere of support and grace.

'The more experienced members of the leadership group are responsible for the mentoring of the other members of the team. This is done in a relatively informal manner and essentially takes the form of a coaching role. Gifts are affirmed and developed as members use them in particular tasks. Preparation assistance is given in a way that facilitates thoughtful creativity. On completion, the performance is evaluated and ways explored to improve what has been done. Action without reflection is only half the work. We seek to ensure that this evaluation happens in a context of affirmation and encouragement, to ensure each person grows through the reflection rather than becoming discouraged and deflated. My perception of coaching is more one of barracking than prescribing.

'In our situation this mentoring is usually short-term, taking place in the lead-up time and during our mission activity. However, some of us are involved in community together throughout the year, which is the best context for this kind of mentoring.

'The task of being a mentor requires that we be teachable and that we extend practical love continually. Any team is made up of both people-focused and task-focused personalities. These people have many different and valid ways of expressing the ministry and doing the work – a variety that God has made and has pooled together for this team and this task. Our job, as leaders and mentors, is to manage and develop both team and task for God's glory and out of our longing for his kingdom.'

———※※※———

STRATEGIES FOR OTHER SITUATIONS

Most, if not all, growing churches have some form of mentoring/discipling program for the purpose of establishing new disciples, bringing members to maturity in Christ and equipping leaders, especially emerging leaders.

We have looked at ways to mentor new disciples and how churches with small groups have built in mentoring strategies for group members and leaders. Here are other significant mentoring strategies and case studies for a variety of other situations.

Each life stage a mentoring opportunity

Life is a series of new beginnings, and each is hard. Every new stage in life is an unknown, unexplored territory and, for many, entered into with trepidation. I well remember the way my wife sought to prepare each of our five children emotionally for their first day at school. (In the middle of the night before commencing school, my most timid child woke to assure me that God was going to be with him!) She then tried to help them de-role each day in busy manses in very demanding parishes by at least asking them how things went. In doing so, June was mentoring them. The same role was exercised to at least some degree for each new phase of their lives. Recently when my eldest grandson was about to go to secondary school, as he and I drove together on an outing, I tried to explain to him something of the challenges and opportunities of this new stage of learning and socialising. We talked about the new temptations he would face and how to try to handle them. I prayed for him in his new situation and when next I saw him, I simply asked him how he was going and we talked briefly. It sounds like something most grandpas would do naturally, but actually it is a form of mentoring!

Pause to think for a moment about some other significant life stages – puberty, our first date, commencing university, entering the workforce, unemployment, leaving home, getting engaged, marriage, our first child, coping with singleness or divorce, middle age, retirement, loss of a partner or life-long friend, to name just a few. Each presents an opportunity to help those entering these new phases to understand what is involved and how to handle it successfully.

At the ELM Centre, the lay training institution I founded and directed in Sydney, we ran short end-of-the-year courses for young people about to enter university or the work force. Courses were led by university lecturers, current or recently graduated university students, business people, trades and crafts people and those working in various other situations. On reflection, the big weakness of our approach was that we didn't encourage churches to select mature people who could accompany the participants and then, with some training, continue mentoring them.

Here are some excellent examples of how support can be provided for some significant stages in life.

Mentoring Youth

Merilyn Smith and Elizabeth Hamilton, Coordinators of the Youth Discipling Program at Scarborough Baptist Church, in Perth, WA, report:

'In the early 1990s, the youth pastor felt there was a need for more mature people to be available to the young people on a one-to-one basis for: discussion of personal problems, encouraging young people in their spiritual walk, and to act as a sounding board for young people. To begin with, it was mainly young male teenagers who were being discipled.

'In 1994 a young woman about to leave high school asked for someone who would be willing to help her learn more about the Bible and its teaching. An older woman, who had some things in common with her, began meeting with her on a weekly basis. They commenced studying the Bible and praying together for specific friends. This young person's love for the Lord and the Bible grew and became infectious. Through her enthusiasm other young people asked to be discipled. More mature Christians offered themselves and were linked with young people with whom they had something in common.

'The program keeps expanding. In May 1998 there were ten disciplers and twenty disciples – some who are discipled by older Christians themselves also disciple younger ones.

'Not only has the program benefited each person spiritually, it has also improved the quality of fellowship across the generations in our church.'

Mentoring Newlyweds

Drs Les and Leslie Parrott are coordinators of the Centre for Relationship Development at Seattle Pacific University, where Les is Professor of Clinical Psychology and Leslie is a marriage and family therapist. They believe that marriage mentoring can be a significant help to building a lifelong marriage.

Their simple 80-page book, *The Marriage Mentor Manual – how you can help the newly-wed couple stay married*[3] has been used widely to help couples strengthen their new marriages through a mentoring relationship. It can be used on its own or as part of a comprehensive marriage preparation program known as *Saving Your Marriage Before It Starts*, for which there is an extensive kit.

Here are some excerpts from the Preface:

'So often we think of a marriage ceremony as the culmination of a courtship process. But, in reality, it is only a beginning. It marks the start of life-long love.

'This small book is an invitation for older married couples to help newly-weds – from the beginning – build unbreakable marital bonds. By following a few of the simple guidelines in this book, and with only a minimal time commitment, you will enrich your own marriage and become a lasting blessing to a couple during their first year of married life together.

'This manual will help you pass on to other couples what God has given to you. It is assumed that if you are using this book, you and your partner have been happily married a number of years. Of course, no marriage is perfect, but being an effective mentor couple does not require perfection. It simply asks that you be who you are.'[4]

The amount of time the couples spend together is not prescribed. They simply recommend a minimum of three meetings throughout the newly-weds' first year together – three, seven and twelve months after the wedding. Clear guidelines are given for each session.

A married couple could learn quickly from this book and take the initiative themselves to offer to meet with newlyweds they feel drawn to.

Churches in the Australian scene that encourage their couples to undertake the *Growing Together in Marriage Program* (or similar marriage group preparation events) could, to good effect, complement that with the above mentoring scheme.

MENTORING AND DEVELOPING EMERGING LEADERS

The following programs for developing emerging leaders incorporate mentoring.

Arrow Leadership Program

This program, which was initiated by Leighton Ford in the United States, has now spread to other countries. The vision is to identify leaders under forty years of age with a proven track record in evangelism. Approximately thirty leaders in each country are invited to join a two-year program which includes two one-week conferences, the completion of a reading list, area peer-cluster gatherings and a mentoring aspect, which is seen as integral to the overall experience. Each participant is expected to meet with an experienced leader in a mentoring relationship, ideally once a month at least for a 9-12 months period initially, then it is hoped that, when one has experienced the value of such a relationship, mentoring will become ongoing.

In Australia, a program with its own unique characteristics based on the original vision, directed by Rev Peter Corney of St Hilary's Anglican Church, Kew, Victoria, has been held successfully and, at the time of writing, the second group of participants is about to graduate.

As Director for Mentoring, I seek to help the participants understand what is involved in this aspect and encourage them to develop a mentoring relationship. By forming a national network among these key emerging leaders across all aspects and denominations of the church, deep friendships are formed and informal peer mentoring takes place. During my travels from state to state, I seek to meet with each participant and have formed on-going mentoring relationships with a significant number of individuals from each of the courses.

The Mayfield Baptist Church

This church, in Newcastle, NSW, launched an exciting and ambitious ministry project aimed at developing the potential of emerging young leaders in the local church. Mentoring is a major facet of the program.

'There are lots of opportunities for young pastors to be trained and equipped for leadership, but often the emerging generation in the local church don't have the same opportunities', Pastor Scott Pilgrim said at its launch in 1996.

'EMERGE aims to tap the potential in our young adult age group and encourage our emerging leaders by providing them with a quality training program and ministry opportunities. Most of them won't stay at Mayfield after their university studies have been completed, so we want to be able to release them prepared to play an active role in the churches they end up in.'

The 'EMERGE' program has four key elements: weekly input sessions for the participants in a wide range of ministry to

164

leadership areas, opportunities to be involved in supervised ministry, a one-on-one mentoring relationship with an older Christian in the church, and practical ministry to reading assignments.

By involving one-on-one mentoring, the program also involves another thirty members of the Mayfield church, each having completed a mentoring equipping program. They meet at least once a fortnight with their 'EMERGE' mentorees.

These relationships are allowing the participants to reflect on the different challenges and opportunities that are arising throughout the program.

Scott Pilgrim said, 'EMERGE was also moving the young participants out of "their comfort zones" by providing them with opportunities to test their gifts in a wide range of areas including preaching, service leading, worship, visitation, pastoral care and work in the local community'.

—✳✳✳—

OTHER EXAMPLES OF MENTORING
A mentoring scheme implemented in a church

Wendell Flentje, the pastor at Belrose Uniting Church in Sydney, undertook a three-year mentoring training program conducted by Les Scarborough of John Mark Ministries. This led him to mentor two young leaders in his church. Later, the elders caught the vision and decided to implement a mentoring strategy to ensure that those who wished to take their discipleship seriously could be cared for in a systematic way.

A stimulating and practical training program led by Les Scarborough, consisting of monthly workshops spread over a year, plus a weekend retreat, involved the twelve elders and ten other leaders.

Most of those who completed the training are now each mentoring one or two mentorees. A small number decided to be mentored themselves before caring for others. To encourage mentors and keep them accountable to the aims of the program, all mentors are encouraged to have their own mentor.

The program is supervised by the pastor and three elders. The three elders meet individually with the pastor for supervision. Each in turn supervises a few mentors. Mentoring is done on a gender basis, with meetings usually monthly, often over a meal or snack. Social activities, sharing in ministry, attendance at training events and other special gatherings together are encouraged.

Wendell commented, 'It is very exciting to observe the enthusiasm and desire to grow in the mentorees, and how this is pushing their mentors to grow themselves. The friendships which are developing through mentoring are a delight to see. The congregation as a whole is becoming more caring and encouraging of one another. This has changed my whole outlook on ministry. I'm in it for life!'

Focusing leaders

The 'Focusing Leaders Program' offered by Church Resource Ministries Australia, which is helping to reshape, redirect and refocus the lives and ministries of many Christian leaders across denominations, has significant mentoring dimensions.

It involves groups of less than twelve participants in approximately one-and-a-half days each month, a retreat for two days and one night, plus home assignments. Reading a comprehensive workbook and completion of work sheets are compulsory preparation for the six-hour monthly meetings. Home assignments also involve the preparation and sharing with each other of the reports and resources that have been useful to each participant.

This work forms the basis for the six-hour monthly meetings that are genuine small-group experiences. Open sharing and prayer are integral parts of these gatherings.

The eight modules or steps for this course cover personal and ministry development. Close relationships, intercessory prayer, openness, accountability and giving and receiving of support are cultivated. One module deals specifically with mentoring and its importance for every leader.

A few of the more mature leaders in the group are trained to mentor two other members. In between each monthly meeting, these leaders meet to coach one-on-one for one-and-a-half hours with those assigned to their care. These coaches first meet with the course facilitator to receive this help themselves.

The two-day retreat is a time for each to share their own journey with the help of a life map they have prepared beforehand.

Significant bonding is forged as levels of trust deepen in an atmosphere of openness and prayer.

The relationships formed in this course generally continue for an extended period and the learning equips leaders to coach and mentor other leaders in their own churches and further afield.

Robert Voigt, a Lutheran pastor from South Australia, who completed this course in 1996, writes:

'At the start of 1996, I was entering my twenty-fifth year in the ministry with a lot of baggage. I was burning out. It was a time of crisis. As I considered all the time and effort I was putting into the ministry to mission of the church and the stress I was experiencing, I wondered whether or not I should look for another line of work.

'God knew I needed a special small group, where I could be ministered to and where I would have lots of opportunity to minister to others. Through this "Focusing Leaders" course, he reshaped, redirected and refocused my life.

'Many pastors are fairly individualistic and lonely. This course changed that forever for me, and for those who did it with me. We realised that we all face similar issues and that we need each other.

'As a result of this course, I now keep regular contact with a number of those who did the course with me and that has been so helpful.'

Woman to Woman

Robyn Claydon, a former deputy-principal at one of Sydney's leading church schools, and now an evangelist and Bible teacher with the international Lausanne movement writes:

'During the last few years in my ministry, I have become increasingly aware of the need to give time to encourage, motivate, empower and equip young Christian women to be all they can be for God. In the course of my ministry throughout the world, I am meeting so many remarkable young women whose hearts are on fire for the Lord, and who are seeking to be used strategically for the Kingdom.

'In order to encourage them I am doing three things. First, taking every opportunity to give them time. This involves talking with them, going for walks, listening to their "heart", asking them what their needs are, determining what further help they need, putting them in touch with people and programs that would be of benefit to them, praying with them and promising ongoing prayer and personal contact if they would like it.

'Second, arranging the occasional Younger Christian Women's Conference, which enables them to go away for a few days, meet with other like-minded young women, receive good Bible teaching and reflect both on the society in which they live and how they can share the Good News of Jesus with those around them.

'Third, in my own home in Sydney, I have a Younger Women's Mentor group that meets every few months for encouragement, sharing, input and prayer. It started with fifteen young women, and in three years grew to sixty! Similar groups have started in other parts of Australia.

'At these meetings, there are always a few older Christian women who can share something of their own experience and act as mentors. In the time between the meetings, there is a lot of informal one-on-one mentoring as some of the young women contact one of the mentors or, often, contact each other. The peer mentoring which results can be extremely helpful.

'Whether Christian women engage in intentional mentoring as I have described, or whether they are always ready to give a word of encouragement to someone else, we are playing an important part in the personal growth and spiritual development of another.'

Churches Mentoring Churches

Where a church plants another church, mentoring of that new congregation is a natural outcome of giving the oversight, support and resources for the fledgling congregation. In many cases the leader of the new group is in a mentoring relationship with the pastor of the mother church and there is a bonding between the new and the original administrative and pastoral bodies. While most planting churches do this task reasonably well, it may bring about a helpful paradigm shift to evaluate and plan this support from the total perspective of mentoring I have sought to present. Matters such as boundaries, co-dependency, freedom to develop a unique identity and expression of ministry, along with regular evaluation, all from a mentoring perspective, should guide the relationship to enable the Holy Spirit to grow the 'plant' in the way he sees fit.

A new movement in church mentoring is fostered by the Teaching Church Network. Lyle E Schaller claims one of the newest and most promising developments in the 1990s is the emergence of 'the self-identified teaching church'. He divides these churches into nine different categories, identifying the teaching church that focuses on developing a mentoring relationship with another church as '. . . the most sophisticated and intensive approach'. It was pioneered by Leith Anderson at Wooddale Church in Eden Prairie, Minnesota, who set up the Teaching Church Network.

According to Paul Borden, Executive Director of TCN, 'A single big event might change minds but it will not effect change. This process of a church mentoring another church will do that.'

While Schaller refers to teaching churches as 'high performance churches' and gives twelve very demanding key requirements for a teaching church, the degree of support one church can give to another, from a mentoring perspective, will vary. It depends upon not only their own performance, but the realistic availability of both ordained and non-ordained leadership to work with the developing church and a host of other issues. However, even evidence of genuine interest, prayer support, encouragement and occasional provision of individuals and teams to share the ministry to assist them in teaching, evaluation and planning will be valuable. While not wanting to diminish this great vision, whatever support is offered must be realistic and manageable.

NOTE FOR TRAINERS OR LEADERS OF MENTORING PROGRAMS

All the information contained in this and the previous segment, *Mentoring a Ministry Team*, could be used as case studies in training events for mentors, or in explaining options for implementing and/or expanding mentoring networks.

—✳✳✳—

IMPLEMENTING A MENTORING SYSTEM

Where mentoring schemes operate in churches, or para-church bodies, they fit somewhere between a highly formalised structured approach and one that may have grown in a totally unorganised manner initially without any clear guidelines or objectives.

The Christian mentoring I have observed in churches has generally started with a pastor or key non-ordained leader taking their discipling role seriously with a few people. They have met with them one-to-one or in a small group to facilitate growth spiritually and equip them for forms of service. This has expanded as others caught the vision.

Early in my ministry, I learnt from experience that Christians who are adequately nurtured, mature in Christ and readily make themselves available to serve him. I became aware of people who had leadership potential and helped them develop their gifts, gave them opportunities to minister and supported and encouraged them. It wasn't until years later I realised I was 'mentoring'. As mentioned earlier, often after conducting a Mentoring Seminar, I find on the completed evaluation forms comments like these: 'I've been mentoring for years and didn't realise it. . .' 'Today has given a name to what I'm already doing'.

Quite apart from whether a formal mentoring structure is in place, pastors and key leaders should undertake disciplemaking as a normal function.

In the section 'Mentoring and Small Groups' (p 150) I explained ways small and large networks use mentoring systems – some quite informal. Here are a few suggestions for introducing a structured system into your church or parish.

MODEL MENTORING YOURSELF

Most significant movements of the Spirit of God commenced in a fairly unspectacular manner. Take the initiative yourself. By doing so you will provide a model in the way you operate and those you help can witness to its effectiveness and begin mentoring others themselves. Practical demonstrations are a good way to help others catch the vision.

GATHER A SMALL GROUP OF POTENTIAL MENTORS

In making your choices, use the criteria for selecting mentors covered in this book. Share your vision with a small number of mature people (some may be relatively young in age) and invite those who respond positively to meet to pray and think together to discern God's intention regarding the possibility of a mentoring system for your church.

Get them reading this and other mentoring books that have influenced you and schedule times to discuss them.

Encourage formation of mentoring relationships among themselves if they are not already in them. Most will probably enter into peer relationships with each other; you may need to mentor one or two yourself.

Undertake training together by participating in good seminars or courses. Use this book to equip your own leaders.

DETERMINE THE AREAS OF NEED

In considering the needs for mentoring in your church, take into account the various life stages that are represented. The first response may be to consider the various age groups. Expand on this by considering people who are entering new stages in their lives, and who would benefit by mentoring from those who understand their new situations, eg young people commencing high school, university, the work force. The unemployed, the newly-marrieds, singles, those moving into more responsible stages in their careers and those retired or about to retire, are further groupings. Don't overlook the singles – unmarried, widowed, divorced. Those who have made recent faith commitments will be another group requiring particular care.

While you won't want to separate out all these categories, it may help you in considering special needs for mentoring.

PLAN TOGETHER

Some or all of the questions at the end of this section will help you in deciding what is appropriate for your situation and how to proceed.

PROMOTION IN THE GATHERED LIFE OF THE CHURCH

This book gives biblical perspectives on mentoring which could be used as resources for a **sermon** series or for studies in the church's regular small groups.

From time to time when opportunities are given for individuals to share their faith stories in regular acts of worship, someone could be asked to tell what it means for them to be in a mentoring relationship. The weekly **news-sheet** is another way to communicate something of the mentoring vision and how it is enriching the church.

Though not 'promotion', it is hoped the church will become familiar with the mentoring program through its regular mention, along with all aspects of the church's life in the **intercessory prayers**.

PAIRING OF MENTORS AND MENTOREES

This ministry is heavily dependent upon rapport and trust. There needs to be some commonality, some areas of common interest, passion, commitment and vision. There also needs to be those link areas, chemistry, the things that make people connect. These are difficult to discern until two people are intentionally in each other's presence.

While suggestions may be made by a senior leader or an oversight group regarding possible pairing, essentially it must be left up to the mentors themselves to pray and follow through hunches about those with whom they should link up. Encourage them to follow the suggestions in the section on 'Finding a Mentor' (p 175).

MENTORS SUPPORT CLUSTERS

Effectiveness will improve if mentors from the various strands of the mentoring system meet together. Most will be busy people so the frequency of these meetings must be realistic. Even infrequent meetings can multiply effectiveness.

These meetings should include: relationship building, reporting progress without disclosure of confidentiality, sharing of ideas and resources and mutual ministry to each other.

Although these clusters are not training sessions, a segment should focus on the development of a skill, revision of some key aspects of recent training or reflection on how new insight resulted in improved effectiveness. Difficulties being encountered should be discussed and successes celebrated.

Suggestions for improving the effectiveness of the scheme could also be discussed. **Prayer** for each other and the scheme should also have a significant place.

SUPERVISION AND SUPPORT

Supervision and support for mentors is an essential aspect of a mentoring system.

Supervision is best provided by a professionally trained carer with a passion for mentoring and who meets the basic qualities expected of all mentors. If such a person is not available, great discernment will be needed in selecting a supervisor who would meet the requirements laid out in Chapter 4.

This person meets with each mentor on a regular basis. With those new to this ministry, the meetings may be every two or three months, becoming less frequent as they gain confidence.

Elsewhere mention is made of the need to know one's limits in mentoring. When mentors are aware that an issue is bigger than their ability to handle it, they should discuss the possibility of seeking more specialised help. The supervisor can then be consulted regarding the specialist resource people who are available.

A SIMPLE PLANNING PROCESS
Determine the 'life stages' groups represented in your church
- What 'life stages' are represented – refer to 'Mentoring New Christians', p 147 and 'Strategies for other Situations', p 160 as well as the above. *(Use a separate piece of chart paper for each. Write the 'stage' at the top, then add the responses to the following, on each sheet.)*

Identify the needs of each life stage group
- What are the specific needs of this group?
- In what ways could mentoring benefit this group?

Identify your resources
- Who are possible mentors with the life experience and qualities that match the needs in one or more of these groupings? *(Use the criteria mentioned in this book as a guide to selecting these people.)*

Where will you begin?
- Should you seek to provide mentoring for all of the 'life stages' represented in your church?
- Should you phase the mentoring, beginning with one or more initially?
        If so, with which should you begin?

Support and supervision
- Who will oversee the program?
- What specialist people can you approach to provide support for the mentors?

Training
- What training will be provided?

Enlistment
- How will you approach possible mentors?

Commencement
- When will you begin?

Promotion
How will you introduce this program to your church?

[1] These can be obtained from John Allison, Redcliffe Uniting Church, 1 Richens Street, Redcliffe 4020, Queensland
[2] ibid.
[3] Dr Les Parrott III and Dr Leslie Parrott, Zondervan, 1995
[4] ibid.

NOTES FOR MENTOREES

FINDING A MENTOR

If you feel the need for a mentor, God is more than likely at work to enrich your life!

If that is so, he has taken the initiative and already prepared someone to meet your needs. However, it will be helpful to take these steps to help you in your search.

Follow Jesus' teaching in Matthew 7:7,8: 'Ask, and it will be given you; seek, and you will find; knock, and the door will be opened for you. For everyone who asks receives, and everyone who seeks finds, and for everyone who knocks, the door will be opened.' Here are some guidelines to follow. These are confident promises that God will answer the requests of his people. However, note that there are some conditions (1 John 5:14,15; Matt 21:21,22).

'Ask': This encourages us to make specific requests from our heavenly Father (v 11). 'Seek': This suggests a diligent search, seriousness in wanting a mentor and a willingness to put effort into finding one. 'Knock': We must take initiatives, approaching people to check their interest and availability.

ASK

Pray expectantly. Mentors have played an important role from the early biblical times – they are part of God's plan. Ask a friend, a relative or an older Christian in your church to pray for you in your search. Be sure to let them know when you are actually approaching someone to have their prayer cover.

SEEK
1. Identify your needs

Think about what help and guidance you are seeking. That may already be quite clear to you; if so, write it down in specific terms. If you find it difficult to identify your needs, talk it over with a peer or a leader. Initially you may be able to state your need only in general terms and your mentor will help you become more specific.

You are really seeking to identify here what is God's intention for your life. To allow God to get your attention, it would be helpful to try to spend time in retreat, where you pray and think through these matters.

Here are three ways to prompt your thinking in endeavouring to discover what you (and God!) want.

Long-term objectives
- Where do I want my life to be in five to ten years?
- What will it take to get there?
- What stands between me and that outcome?
- What will help me?

Basic areas of life
Ask the following questions of these basic categories of your life: friendships, marriage, family, spiritual life, ministry, work, involvement in the community at large.

Where are your chronic problem areas?
- Where do you need to grow?
- Where do you feel inadequate?
- Where and how are you experiencing repeated failure?

Four levels of competency
- In what ways do you want to **increase your knowledge and understanding**?
- What **attitudes or values** do you feel the need to cultivate?
- What **habits and behaviours** are you trying to establish or change?
- What **skills** do you wish to develop?[1]

This exercise is meant to help you find specific areas where you need help. The list you make may need to be prioritised and the top one or more chosen on which to commence work. However, your mentor may be helped if he/she reads your full list.

2. Select some potential mentors

Make an optimistic list. Don't hesitate to list those whom you may at first consider to be most unlikely to help. At this stage you are 'dreaming', just gathering a list to think further about. Your creative thinking will be hindered if you pause to analyse each name initially.

Reflect on past or present relationships. List those who enabled you to:
• grow personally and spiritually
• develop your ministry
• find direction in your life and work.

Add to your list people with whom you have not had a close relationship previously, but who have impressed you by their life and witness. To begin with, consider people in these areas:
• in your church
• in other churches
• people you have met at various events – seminars, retreats, conferences, etc
• people in the Christian networks of which you are part – organisations, movements, associations, etc
• speakers, preachers, educators who have impressed you.

Using the work sheet at the end of this section, list these names.

3. Evaluate your list

Read 'The Basic Qualities of a Mentor', p 64.

Select those that you think fit most of these. (For those whom you don't know well, this will be difficult, but follow your general impressions.)

Indicate this in the second column on your work sheet – you may do this by giving each a 1-8 rating, or just an 'X'.

4. Match to your needs

Match your potential mentors with one or more needs with which you think they may be able to help you.

Write the needs in the third column.

Comment: This may seem a long process but it will be worth the effort. However, God often surprises us, and our needs and possible mentors quickly come into focus without this effort.

KNOCK

Contact the person at the top of your list. Don't prejudge their availability – often it will be a very busy person who surprises you by responding positively.

State briefly and clearly your purpose in contacting them – 'I wonder if I could meet with you to talk over the possibility of you being my mentor? Could I take you for a meal or coffee?'

One of my mentorees commenced his approach to me with, 'I have observed you over the years and I'm impressed that as an older minister you still love Jesus and that's how I want to be when I get to your age, so could you consider being my mentor?' Now there's a way to go! At least it suggests that some genuine affirmation first is a good way to commence.

FURTHER SUGGESTIONS

Follow up on offers of help. I frequently say to emerging leaders with whom I am impressed, 'Don't hesitate to contact me if you think I can be of help'. Follow up on such offers from those you meet.

Use a referral approach. Once you have identified a possible mentor whom you don't know personally, seek to find a person in their network who could give you an introduction. It may be suggested that you may use their name or they may phone them personally to recommend you.

Talk to key leaders at special events. It is often said that some of the richest benefits from conferences and the like come from contacts made in the corridors. Seek out speakers and other key leaders at these events. Affirm and discuss briefly something that was said which was helpful, or seek their advice. This can be done by talking where you meet them or by making an appointment to speak to them later over a meal or a walk together. Conclude the time by asking if they mind you contacting them occasionally to discuss matters or seek their advice. If they are positive, be sure to get their card. This could lead to an occasional or a more intensive mentoring relationship.

BEWARE OF THE OBSTACLES

Be alert to the barriers which will block your search for a mentor. One or two have already been mentioned, eg **'don't be deterred by a person's busyness'**.

Procrastination. Someone has said, 'The road to hell is paved with good intentions!' To save yourself being dilatory, put your work in this section in a time frame – set deadlines. You may want to tell a friend so that they can encourage you to act.

Being deterred by time demands. Yes! there will be time involved in travel, meeting together and working through your agreed assignments, but the final outcome will be well worth the investment.

Distance. If you live at a distance, which prevents regular face-to-face meetings, most of your communication will be by phone or e-mail. But be sure to ask if you can meet when your mentor is visiting your area.

Fear of transparency. A good mentor will sometimes ask you hard questions. As your level of trust grows, and it may take some time, the freedom to be open and honest will increase. The end product is worth any pain!

Unwillingness to be accountable. In our day and age in most of western culture, doing your own thing is the flavour of the age. Independence is not what Christianity is about. Community, interdependence, togetherness, are major themes in the New Testament. Paul's teaching on the church as a body is a splendid illustration of this (Rom 12:3-8; 1 Cor 12:12-27). Those who hedge accountability to one another most probably find it difficult to own Jesus Christ as their Lord in the fullest sense of the New Testament teaching.

THE FIRST MEETING WITH YOUR MENTOR

Not every leader will understand what is involved in mentoring, so you may want to give them a copy of this book to read before you meet, or even before they commit themselves to the first meeting.

Keep in mind that your first meeting is exploratory, you will talk over the possibility of this relationship. Both of you will need to feel some initial bonding, a good feeling, when you first meet.

Give some thought to questions the mentor might ask in getting to know you. See the section, Questions for the First Session in 'Asking Good Questions', p 124.

First impressions are important. Be dressed appropriately. Be on time. Take your diary and notepaper. If they are an older person and not a close acquaintance, greet them with some degree of respect, using Mrs, Dr, Pastor, Mr, etc. Let them take the initiative to tell you to call them by their Christian name.

Be clear about the help you think you need. Ask them how they would like you to contact them in future – some may prefer to be contacted through their office phone or by e-mail. If so, check whether they mind you contacting them at home in an emergency. Record these details.

If this meeting takes place over a meal or coffee, insist on paying if you are in a position to do so. While I frequently meet these expenses myself for a first meeting, and continue to do so when my mentoree is unable, many mentors have limited finances.

If the initial reactions of each of you are positive, then you will need to agree upon frequency of meetings, the initial period for which you will meet, accountability and other matters. (See 'More Guidelines for Mentors', p 137, for ideas here.) Be clear about the date and venue of your next meeting.

Not all these first meetings are positive. Each of you may need to think and pray about it further, or it may be clear that you are not meant to form the relationship.

WORKSHEET

Statement of the help and guidance I seek

_____

_____

_____

Potential Mentors	Qualities	Needs They Could Meet

Those I will approach (and when):

_____

_____

_____

—✳✳✳—

Being a Good Mentoree

Here are some suggestions to help you to be a good mentoree.

What mentors look for

Mentors expect certain things from their mentorees that encourage them to maintain the relationship:

Teachable spirit

Mentors should never come across as know-it-alls and they certainly don't want that attitude in those they are seeking to help, though their mentorees will often be ahead of them in various ways. They look for a humble openness to learn. Most mentors readily acknowledge that it is a learning experience for them also.

Ability to reflect

Throughout the whole of this book, there is a strong emphasis upon reflection as integral to transformation. Your mentor will help you become more reflective by the questions he/she asks you. If you are using the study guides in this book, the 'Personal Reflection' segments will be helpful in this regard. Journalling also plays an important part in this process, so although people vary in the way they journal, you will be expected to be diligent in your efforts.

Performance

Mentors lose interest in mentorees who don't take the relationship seriously – who repeatedly, without sound reasons, don't do the things they agreed to do. Mentors look for an **eagerness to learn, courage to take risks, a growing maturity and readiness to take responsibility**. Attitude and actions are important. Mentors enjoy seeing mentorees growing personally and spiritually. They also are encouraged by their mentoree's growth in knowledge and understanding, not only that gained from them, but by following up suggestions or taking initiatives themselves. Mentors will discourage irresponsibility, but be inspired by strong faith that moves their mentorees into deep uncharted waters. Then they are there to rescue if necessary.

Growth in spirituality

Emphasis upon spiritual development is a common theme in this book. Mentors don't look for unreal piety, but they are encouraged when the basic spiritual disciplines are taken seriously and progress becomes evident. Take seriously the building up of your prayer base. Begin with just one or two and keep working on it. One of my best mentorees told me it took some months to take this seriously and she now sees it as the backbone of her ministry.

Responsibility

Dependency will be discouraged. Being responsible for one's own actions will be encouraged. Mentorees should own their attitudes and their behaviour and deal with these aspects appropriately. Mentors like to see their charges lead as leaders, being good team builders and knowing how to be answerable and accept that 'the buck stops' with them.

Reliability

Mentors are usually busy people so be on time for appointments. Seek to meet deadlines and pursue excellence in what you do.

Appreciation

Mentors need to be affirmed and encouraged. Occasionally send a 'thank you' note and/or a small inexpensive gift. (One mentoree gave me a jar of honey from their beehive. Each time I dipped into it, I remembered that mentoree!) Include them on your Christmas mailing list. Birthdays and wedding anniversaries and other special events bring joy when remembered. If you are in a situation where you are answerable to a governing body, from time to time report on the role your mentor plays in your ministry. Occasionally, suggest a letter of appreciation be sent to your mentor and/or the group to whom he/she is answerable. Sensitively affirm your mentors publicly when the occasion presents itself.

OTHER THINGS TO DO
Celebrate surprises!

Make a special phone call or arrange a meeting to report anything that would encourage your mentor. For example, how well an interview with a potential employer went, acceptance for a new position, a difficult situation with a good outcome – any of the things you discussed at depth and prayed about together. Some serendipity is always a joy.

Ask for extra support

When a crisis or difficult situation arises in between regular meetings, don't hesitate to phone/fax to ask your mentor for advice and prayer support.

Have your mentor meet those close to you

Arrange a meal with your close friend or spouse. Organise a meal with your family so he/she can put a face to those who answer the phone! Offer accommodation if convenient, should he/she visit your area.

Introduce your mentor to your workplace

One mentoree invited me to have a meal in the staff dining room at his business so that I could see his work environment and meet some of his colleagues. Those who are church leaders often ask me to meet their staff, either socially or to consult with them, and therefore gain a greater understanding of the mentoree's work environment.

Keep your mentor up-to-date

Inform your mentor promptly of any changes to your phone numbers, e-mail, address, etc. It can save him/her time and ensure you are readily accessible.

Meet costs if possible

Costs of meals and coffees can be beyond a mentor's means, so offer to meet these if you are able. Alternatively, bring a cut lunch or snack to share with your mentor in a park or their office. Some whose full-time ministry is coaching or mentoring have to charge to cover their time and expenses. Many mentors do this work as an adjunct to their regular ministry, which meets their costs. Others, particularly retired people, have expenses that should be reimbursed. Some churches are so aware of the advantage of this support for their staff that they allow for it in their budget. Don't take another's availability and generosity for granted. Discuss the matter with them and at least try to cover their out-of-pocket expenses.

Pastor your mentors

In the upper room, on the night of his betrayal, Jesus said to his disciples, 'You are those who stood by me in my trials' (Luke 22:28). He affirmed the support he had received from his followers. When your mentors are under stress, show concern in a sensitive manner. I remember mentoring while going through a most difficult period. The strain showed and my mentoree offered to pray and gave words of encouragement. I was deeply moved and blessed. Of course, mentors need to be willing to receive. Some may find that difficult, so don't be discouraged, include them in your private prayers and maybe a brief note may be appropriate.

STUDY GUIDE

PERSONAL REFLECTION

1. How do you feel when working with a person who doesn't have a 'teachable spirit', or is unreliable?
   - In what ways do you show you are teachable and reliable?
2. Think of a recent occasion when someone showed their appreciation of you.
   - How did they do it?
   - How did it make you feel?
3. What happened on any occasions where you sought to pastor a leader quite senior to you?
   - What did you learn from that?

GROUP WORK

1. Share your personal reflections.
2. In what ways other than those listed, could appreciation be expressed to a mentor?
3. Discuss the matter of costs.
4. What other things can help mentorees maximise their mentoring experience for themselves and their mentors?

---

[1] This is an adaptation and summary from *As Iron Sharpens Iron*, Howard and William Hendricks, Moody, 1995

APPENDIX

OTHER ISSUES FOR MENTORS

Greg and Meryem Brown have designed a *Spiritual Director's Issues Guide*[1] specifically for people in ministry. The intention is to supply some starting points for exploring issues that affect the minister's person, relationships and ministry, as well as his/her emotional, physical and spiritual health. Clearly not all of these questions could be asked at a single sitting. (However, they should probably all be asked over a period of time.) We suggest they be used as a guide to indicate specific areas of need; the spiritual director should then supplement the list to open up and deal with the relevant issues. Especially courageous ministering people receiving direction, and/or those becoming more comfortable with their shadow side, could indicate to their spiritual guide the particular questions which ought to be asked regularly.

1. Sub-personal – basic needs, drives and reactions

1.1   Describe the last time you had a really good laugh.

1.2   In what types of situations are you likely to experience feelings of jealousy or resentment? What do you do with those feelings?

1.3   In what situations are you likely to feel like criticising others?

1.4   Describe how you deal with sexual fantasies, and feelings of sexual temptation.

1.5   Describe the last time you felt angry or aggressive.

1.6   How does your desire to assert yourself or control situations express itself in an inappropriate way?

1.7   How do you deal with the temptation to expect/demand perfection in yourself?

1.8   When do you experience guilt? What do you do with the guilt feelings?

1.9   How do you know you are getting sufficient sleep and rest?

1.10 When was your last full day off and how did you spend it?

1.11 How would your doctor react to your diet?

1.12 How would you rate your exercise/recreation/leisure/hobbies out of ten?

1.13 Are you conscious of any undealt-with loss or grief?

1.14 Have you recently experienced depressive thoughts and/or feelings?

1.15 Are you getting any messages through your dreaming?

1.16 In what ways are you experiencing/expressing your connectedness with the earth and the rest of the created order?

1.17 How do you satisfy the need to create something?

1.18 When was the last time you experienced meaningful, positive closure?

1.19 What new understanding(s) about yourself have you become aware of recently?

2. Inter-personal – community and intimacy needs

2.1 In what ways are you consciously developing friendship/mateship/intimacy with your partner?

2.2 How would your partner rate the sexual intimacy within your relationship?

2.3 How would family members other than your partner know that developing intimacy with them is one of your primary goals?

2.4 Describe the last time you intentionally spent time with someone (outside your family) who enjoys your company rather than needs you.

2.5 What relationships are you developing that encourage you to move toward deeper levels of honesty, vulnerability and accountability?

2.6 Are you aware of any inappropriate aspects of any relationships in which you are currently involved?

2.7 Do you feel uncomfortable about any aspect of your same-sex relationships?

2.8 Are there any people in your life whom you may need to forgive?

2.9 Are there any people in your life whom you feel owe you an apology?

2.10 How good are you at maintaining an appropriate balance between giving and receiving?

2.11 When did you last spend quality time with a person not connected with the church? What did you learn?

3. Supra-personal – spiritual needs

3.1   Describe the most significant aspect of your relationship with God.

3.2   How much time are you regularly allowing for meditation and reflection on spiritual issues?

3.3   What is the best way for you to address your spiritual formation and/or direction?

3.4   Are you aware of any issues in your life for which you should seek forgiveness from God?

3.5   Is there any sense of unresolved pain or hurt in your life which could be resolved by you forgiving God?

3.6   What new understanding about God have you become aware of recently?

3.7   How have you been conscious of God at work in your life recently?

3.8   When did you last read something from a theological perspective with which you are not comfortable? From another faith? What did you learn?

4. Ministerial – handling the ministry role

4.1   How successful have you been at ensuring that your primary focus is on serving God rather than serving God's people?

4.2   How successful have you been at balancing the conflicting and competing demands of ministry?

4.3   How have you coped with the expectations of others that you have not been able to fulfil?

4.4   Given that we all operate behind masks or a persona to some degree or another, are you basically happy or unhappy with the amount of time you live on that level?

4.5   How successful have you been recently at applying truths from your preaching/teaching to your own life?

4.6   What is the most effective way for you to debrief, ie, what is your decompression routine?

4.7   Are there any ways in which your time management/goal-setting/task prioritisation could be improved?

4.8   In what ways are you working outside your area of gifting?

4.9   Are there any tasks you are currently responsible for which could/should be delegated, or for which you ought to be training another person?

4.10 Are you regularly allowing time for reflection, dreaming, visioning and medium/long-term planning?

4.11 In what ways are you satisfying your need for intellectual stimulation?

4.12 When was the last time you evaluated your current training and personal development needs?

4.13 What has been the most satisfying ministry experience you have had in the last week? In the last month? In the last year?

—***—

RENOVARÉ SELF-EXAMINATION QUESTIONS

Here are some questions developed by Richard Foster for **Renovaré** groups which can be helpful, especially in co-mentoring. (See Chapter 6, p 150, *Mentoring and Small Groups*.)

They are based on the five spiritual dimensions that we see in the early church and later movements:

Contemplative:	The Prayer-filled Life
Holiness:	The Virtuous Life
Charismatic:	The Spirit-empowered Life
Social Justice:	The Compassionate Life
Evangelical:	The Word-centred Life

When all five of these traditions are active in the church, they bring balance and wholeness to the Christian life and mission.

These form the basis of the Renovaré group covenant. Mutual accountability helps maximise this group agreement, facilitating balance and wholeness under the guidance and empowerment of the Holy Spirit.

The manual is *A Spiritual Formation Group Workbook* and the major resource is the *Devotional Classics*.

The following questions were asked weekly in the context of a loving and supportive small-group fellowship that is committed to living the **Renovaré Covenant**. The individuals in such a fellowship pray for one another bringing the mercy, forgiveness, nurture, care and support of the Lord. Where a group experience is not possible, individuals use these questions for weekly self-examination, confession and prayer.

1. The Prayer-filled Life

- What experiences of prayer and meditation have you had this week?

- What difficulties or frustrations did you encounter?
- What joys and delights? (Phil 4:6,7; Eph 6:18; 1 Thess 5:16-18; Matt 14:23; Ps 119:97)

2. The Virtuous Life
- What temptations did you face this week?
- How did you respond?
- What is your determination for the future? (1 Cor 10:13; Heb 4:15,16; James 1:13-15)

3. The Spirit-empowered Life
- What movements of the Holy Spirit did you experience this week?
- What fruit of the Spirit would you like to see increase in your life? (Gal 5:22; 1 Thess 5:19-21; Luke 3:16; 1 Cor 14:1; Eph 4:11-13; 1 Tim 4:14)

4. The Compassionate Life
- What opportunities to serve others have you had this week?
- How did you respond?
- Were you able to work for justice and shalom? (Gal 2:10; Amos 2:7; Luke 4:18,19; Matt 12:18-21; Luke 10:25-37)

5.The Word-centred Life
- In what ways have you encountered Christ in your study of the Bible this week?
- How has it shaped you?
- In what ways did God open the way for you to share your faith? (Deut 6:4-8; Acts 17:11; 1 Tim 4:13; 2 Tim 3:15; Col 3:16)

ACCOUNTABILITY QUESTIONS FOR LIFE TRANSFORMATION GROUPS[3]
(See *'Mentoring and Small Groups'*, Chapter 6, p 150, where Life Transformation Groups are introduced.)
These Accountability Questions are to be asked of one another in a weekly meeting of accountability which values honesty, confidentiality and integrity (Prov 27:17; James 5:16; Gal 6:1-5).

These questions are only as helpful as you are willing to be honest and vulnerable.

1.Did you finish the reading and hear from God?
 • What are you going to do about it?
2.Have you been a testimony this week to the greatness of our Lord Jesus Christ with both your words and actions?
3.Have you had inappropriate thoughts about someone who is not your spouse, or been exposed to sexually alluring material?
4.Have you lacked any integrity in your financial dealings or coveted something which does not belong to you?
5.Have your lived with your spouse in an understanding way and been pro-active in your child's development?
6.Have you damaged another person by your words, either behind their back or face to face?
7.Have you succumbed to a personal addiction?
 • Explain.
 • Have you continued to remain angry toward another?
 • Have you secretly wished for another's misfortune so that you might excel?
 • Have you been completely honest with me?

'Therefore, confess your sins to one another, and pray for one another, so that you may be healed.' (James 5:16)

[1] Prepared by Greg and Meryem Brown of **synergia**©, PO Box 23 Kippa-Ring Qld 4021 – Phone 907 3889 5666. Originally titled, *Spiritual Director's Issues Guide*, ©, used by permission.
[2] Both are by Richard Foster and James Bryan Smith and were published by Harper, San Francisco, in 1993.
[3] © 1992–1995 – Robert E Logan and Neil Cole – used by permission.

TRAINER'S NOTES

PRIOR CONSIDERATIONS

LEADING THIS TRAINING

Facilitating this learning will demand both time and effort. You will not only plan to give time to preparation for the group meetings but as a learner along with the group you are expected to be involved in all aspects of the course. You will be part of the learning process. It will require dedication on your part and humility to be a learner among learners.

Your role will be that of enabler, facilitator, not that of teacher or lecturer. Part of this role will involve you in taking a clear lead at appropriate points.

Understanding the learning process, sensitivity, willingness to listen, an ability to enable learners and a living, growing Christian experience are essential. Read carefully 'How Adults Learn', Chapter 5, p 104).

There is a strong emphasis upon modelling in this book. A crucial test of the leadership of this training will be how the aspects discussed are demonstrated by the facilitator. We communicate far more by modelling with our lives than we do by what we say.

THEOLOGICAL FRAMEWORK

This book gives a biblical and theological framework for understanding mentoring. Jesus provides the prime example of how to mentor effectively. Therefore there are frequent attempts to understand how Jesus went about developing his followers as both disciples and potential leaders. The proposed training program seeks to mix the sections of the book so that the biblical facts and truths are part of most sessions.

One of the main aims of the book, and hopefully any training based upon it, is that which guides all authentic Christian education – that participants will understand and meet with the risen Christ and see how he went about his ministry, of which ours is an extension.

REFLECTIVE LEARNING

While there is much content in this book to be studied, the underlying educational method is to create an environment of discovery using reflective learning so that, under the Spirit's prompting, participants will more effectively come to understand and grow through their individual and group experiences. Ensure you understand the section 'How Adults Learn'.

PARTICIPANTS' PREPARATION

The effectiveness of this course design is dependent upon a commitment from each participant that they will complete their individual work prior to each session. This is the foundation for the learning, so if a number come unprepared, the training will be diminished in effectiveness. This individual work negates the need for lectures and ensures the gathered learning is experience-based – a most stimulating and effective way to learn!

TIME COMMITMENT
Home assignments
The individual work, to be completed at home, in most cases will take **less than two hours** for all the sections covered in each training session.
Training sessions
Each session, as shown under 'A Design for Mentoring Sessions' will require **two hours** (Chapter 5, p 144).

WHERE TO RUN THE TRAINING

Choose a quiet comfortable environment for both the evening seminars and the intensive weekend learning experience. Depending upon the number participating, a home or a small 'training room' in a church building would be suitable for the evening seminars, provided it can be heated or cooled when necessary.

As there will be movement in and out of different-sized clusters in each session, the seating will need to allow for this.

RESOURCES
Each participant will require:
- A copy of this book
- An exercise book for notes and journalling
- Bible

Facilitators will need:
- A copy of this book
- Bible
- Whiteboard and whiteboard markers (and/or) chart paper, a clip board and texta pens
- Overhead projector and screen (plus extension lead and table), if visuals are to be used, especially in the first session, to summarise the contents of Chapter 1.

To improve facilitation skills

My Small Group Manual, *The Small-Group Leader*, Openbook, 1996, gives helpful guidance on effective small-group leadership, understanding and helping group participants and enabling healthy group life.

People Skills by Robert Bolton, Simon & Schuster, Aust, 1989, is a useful communication-skills handbook to make groups more productive.

Covenant

The Group Covenant found at the end of these notes seeks to obtain from each participant the commitment to prior individual preparation and full participation in the group sessions.

In an endeavour to gain this commitment in the first session, explain its purpose, basing your comments on the section dealing with accountability, under 'Walking the Road Together', Chapter 2, p 34. Then discuss the proposed covenant. It can be modified to suit your group's situation. Some will want to alter, subtract or add to it.

Training Sessions

Proposed Training Program

1. Orientation Session
   Introducing Mentoring (Chapter 1)
2. Christian Mentoring and Disciplemaking
   The Need for Mentoring
   Major Areas for Mentoring
3. An Adequate Idea of God
   The Heart of Christian Mentoring

4. Having a Sane Estimate of Ourselves and Others
   Sharpening our Self-Awareness
5. Walking the Road Together
   Mentoring as a Dynamic System
   Peer Mentoring
6. Biblical Mentoring Models
   Basic Qualities of a Mentor
7. The Crucial Role of Prayer
   How Adults Learn
   Journalling
8. Using the Bible – Our Prime Mentoring Resource
   The Main Roles of a Mentor
9. Mentoring Styles
   Setting Boundaries
10. Asking Good Questions
    Active Listening
    More Guidelines for Mentors
11. Dispelling Some Myths
    Our Personal Mentoring Resources
    Beginning as a Mentor
12. A Design for Mentoring Sessions
    Mentoring New Christians
    Mentoring and Small Groups
13. Finding a Mentor
    Being a Good Mentoree

This outline is only a proposal; adapt it to suit your own situation.

A basic course should include the first eleven sessions. Sessions 12 and 13 could be covered a short while later in evening seminars or the separate themes dealt with as part of the in-service learning segments in the mentors' support cluster meetings.

Session 13 could be combined with a few of the earlier segments as a program especially for mentorees.

SUGGESTED BASIC COURSE DESIGN FOR A CHURCH
• **Three weekly or bi-weekly two-hour evening seminars** covering Sessions 1–3.

- **Intensive weekend-away event**

Friday evening	– Arrival and fellowship
Saturday	– 8.30 am to 10.30 am – Session 4
	– 11.00 am to 1.00 pm – Session 5
	– 1.00 pm to 3.30 pm – Lunch and free time
	– 3.30 pm to 5.30 pm – Session 6
	– Evening Fellowship
Sunday	– 8.30 am to 10.30 am – Session 7
	– 11.00 am to 1.00 pm – Session 8

(NB: Sessions 7 and 8 cover Prayer and Bible Study, and both include worship dimensions.)

- **Three weekly or bi-weekly two-hour evening seminars** covering Sessions 9–11.

(Make a copy of the full program with dates, themes and venues, for each participant.)

ORIENTATION SESSION DESIGN
Praise segment *(10 mins)*
Work in pairs
Sharing *(5 mins)* What are your hopes and expectations for this course?
Prayer *(8 mins)* What is your greatest personal need for which I could pray?

What is your greatest need to enable you to make the most of this learning experience?

LEADER'S INTRODUCTION
Briefly cover some of these items from Chapter 1, 'Introducing Mentoring'.
- **Its origin and meaning** – give brief introduction to this, then give each pair two or three of the words from the definition to brainstorm their understanding of these and their relevance. Get brief feedback from the whole group.
- **Part of the fabric of life** – Think of a creative way to summarise this, using visuals, etc, possibly enlisting someone beforehand to do all or part of the presentation.

- **It works!** – Three good readers could read these. Better still, those who have benefited from mentoring sessions themselves could briefly tell their experience. (You may want to use overhead transparency copies of the diagrams in the section 'Mentoring as a Dynamic System', Chapter 3, p 50 to introduce this segment.)
- **You can do it!** – Read 1 Cor 1:26-31 with some brief comments.

Agreement to the covenant – Explain we are looking for a serious commitment – but in a framework of grace!

Prayer in small groups for the course, the facilitator and participants and the future of mentoring undertaken.

RUNNING THE SESSIONS

Timing of group sessions. The times given are for the leader's guidance and may be varied. Each session has been designed to last for approximately two hours. The times taken will vary according to the size of the group. Although the times are only a guide, it is important to remain within the suggested time-frame wherever possible.

Main items to cover. The study guides at the end of each segment in this book under *Small Group Work* (also *In Pairs*) give suggestions for main items to be covered in each training session. These are placed in this position so participants know what to expect and see the relevance of their individual work for the training.

Make your own session plan, based on the *Small Group Work* segment, including time for worship and prayer.

Work in clusters. Most of the learning is done in pairs or in clusters of four to six (no more). Be sure everyone understands what is expected of the work in clusters. If you have more than six participants, appoint a competent small-group leader to guide each group. Try to keep yourself free to move around the groups to ensure there is good participation and that they are keeping to the subject.

Use your knowledge of the group when creating these sub-groups of twos or threes so that they will work well together.

Group leaders should understand the topic under discussion and have a good grasp of group dynamics.

Encourage each person to participate freely, but don't coerce people. Enable people to listen to each other. Strive for equal participation and equal sharing of the time available. Prevent any from dominating. Encourage tolerance of opposing views. Make each feel significant and of worth. Do not be afraid of silences. Silence is often the occasion of our deepest thinking and self-examination.

Relationship building is an essential aspect of the learning experience. Levels of trust will need to be developed before people will feel free to be open in their sharing.

Plenary segments. After most work in clusters, it will be appropriate to get some feedback and allow time for questions and discussion.

Closure of each session. All learning should lead to action. Allow time to tie together the themes. Then use a closing reflection where each can think about what they have learnt and feel they should be doing. Simply ask, 'What have we learnt in this session and how can we apply it to when we mentor, and in our life and ministry now?' Encourage participants to make notes in their journals of this proposed action. This is probably best done in pairs so that it can lead into prayer for one another.

THE ROLE OF PRAYER IN THE TRAINING

Prayer receives a strong emphasis in this book. Its importance cannot be overstated. Make prayer an important dimension of each session. This will model the reliance upon God and awareness of the Spirit's presence and power which is at the heart of successful mentoring.

To commence. Commence each session with prayer in pairs. The questions used to commence this segment in the orientation session can be repeated or have participants simply ask, 'What can I pray for you now?' Encourage thanksgiving as well as intercession.

To conclude. The sessions should end with prayer in pairs or each praying for the person on his or her left in the small group.

During the session. Encourage prayer when appropriate.

Between meetings. The covenant encourages the participants to pray for each other between meetings.

FURTHER NOTES
THE EXTENSIVE WEEKEND AWAY
   While this allows for a substantial amount of learning during this period, it will also create a sense of community which will be a good foundation for the ongoing Mentors Support Cluster, referred to in Chapter 6 under 'Implementing a Mentoring System', p 169. A substantial amount of individual preparation will be necessary for the five sessions, so the overall program will need to allow for this, possibly by allowing a gap prior to the weekend.

EVALUATION
   Undertake **informal** evaluation after most of the sessions by asking all or a few participants, 'How did you find the session?', 'What's been helpful in the way we are doing things?' 'Is there anything we can do better – or differently?'
   At the conclusion of the program, do some **formal** evaluation. This can best be done by having participants complete an evaluation form which allows for comments on what was found helpful, what could be done differently, what was unhelpful, what further help they would appreciate, the effectiveness of the leadership and general comments. This information will be useful for future training events.

CONCLUSION OF TRAINING
   Prepare a closure experience to finish the training, using some of the suggestions made under Learn to Let Go in 'Setting Boundaries', Chapter 5, p 116.

GROUP COVENANT

Because of the high expectation of those undertaking the training, the following covenant, to which each participant should agree, will enable maximum benefit from the learning.

A covenant in biblical terms, unlike a contract, is an agreement hedged around by grace and not law. Below is a statement of intention and hope. It is dependent upon God's enabling grace.

1. I will endeavour to give priority in my weekly program to each aspect of this course – home studies and group meetings.

2. I will pray for each of my fellow group members and the mentoring ministry of my local church.

3. I will endeavour to be as open as I know how in my sharing.

4. I will participate in the group meetings but not dominate.

5. I will seek to deepen my own relationship with God through personal Bible reading, silent reflection and prayer.

6. I agree to hold in trust all that is shared of a confidential nature.

7. I will seek to enable the group to become a caring fellowship by listening to each person and giving encouragement and support.

Selected Bibliography

In addition to those titles already referred to, the following is a representative selection of resources consulted.

Adsit, Christopher B *Personal Disciplemaking*, Thomas Nelson, 1993

Barry, William A & Connolly, William J *The Practice of Spiritual Direction*, Harper & Row, 1982

Biehl, Bobb *Mentoring*, Broadman & Holman, 1996

Cloud, Dr Henry & Townsend, Dr John *Boundaries*, Strand Publishing, 1992

Covey, Steven R *The Seven Habits of Highly Effective People*, Simon & Schuster, 1989

Crabb, Dr Larry and Allender, Dr Dan *Encouragement – The Key to Caring*, Strand Publishing, 1984

Crabb, Dr Larry *The Silence of Adam*, Zondervan, 1995

Foley, Griff (ed) *Understanding Adult Education and Training*, Allen & Unwin, 1995

Green, Michael & Stevens, R Paul *New Testament Spirituality*, Eagle, 1994

Grey, John *Men Are from Mars, Women Are from Venus*, Thorsons, 1993

Hendricks, Howard & William *As Iron Sharpens Iron*, Moody, 1995

Jeff, Gordon *Spiritual Direction for Every Christian*, SPCK, 1987

Krallmann, Gunter *Mentoring for Mission*, Jensco, Hong Kong & Globe Europe Missions, 1992

Leadership, Summer 1996

Leech, Kenneth *Soul Friend*, Harper & Row, 1980

MacLennan, Nigel *Coaching and Mentoring*, Gower, 1995

Ogne, Steven L & Nebel, Thomas P *Empowering Leaders through Coaching*, Direction Ministry Resources, 1995

Parrott III, Dr Les & Parrott, Dr Leslie *The Marriage Mentor Manual*, Zondervan, 1995

Shea, Gordon F *Mentoring – A Practical Guide*, Crisp Publications, 1992

Smith, James Bryan *A Spiritual Formation Workbook*, Harper, 1989

202

Stanley, Paul D & Clinton, J Robert *Connecting*, Navpress, 1992
Van Atta, Lucibel *Women Encouraging Women*, Multnomah Press, 1987
Vanderwall, SJ, Francis W *Spiritual Direction*, Paulist Press, 1981
Walling, Terry B *Focusing Leaders*, CRM Publishing, 1994
Whittaker, Mike and Cartwright, Ann *32 Activities on Coaching & Mentoring*, Gower, 1997

INDEX